by **Fumi Yoshinaga**

VOL. **19**

TABLE *of* CONTENTS

THE INNER CHAMBERS

CAST *of* CHARACTERS

From the birth of the "inverse Inner Chambers" to its zenith, to eradicating the Redface Pox, and now to the end of Tokugawa rule...?

SENIOR CHAMBERLAIN

LADY KASUGA

↓

MADE-NOKO-JI ARIKOTO (SIR O-MAN)

TOKUGAWA IEMITSU (III)

Impersonated her father, Iemitsu, at Lady Kasuga's urging after he died of the Redface Pox. Later became the first female shogun.

TOKUGAWA TSUNAYOSHI (V)

TOKUGAWA TSUNASHIGE

TOKUGAWA IETSUNA (IV)

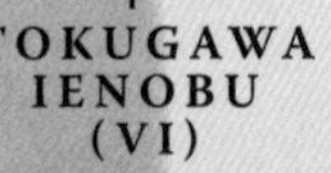

TOKUGAWA IENOBU (VI)

SENIOR CHAMBERLAIN

EMONNOSUKE

TOKUGAWA IETSUGU (VII)

SENIOR CHAMBERLAIN

EJIMA

PRIVY COUNCILLOR

MANABE AKIFUSA

PRIVY COUNCILLOR

YANAGISAWA YOSHIYASU

PRIVY COUNCILLOR

KANO HISAMICHI

TOKUGAWA YOSHIMUNE (VIII)

Third daughter of Mitsusada, the second head of the Kii branch of the Tokugawa family. Acceded to domain lord and then, upon the death of Ietsugu, to shogun. Imposed and lived by a strict policy of austerity, dismissing large numbers of Inner Chambers courtiers and pursuing policies designed to increase income to the treasury.

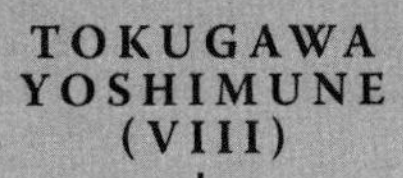

TOKUGAWA YOSHIMUNE (VIII)

MUNETADA

TOKUGAWA HARUSADA

TOKUGAWA IENARI (XI)

TOKUGAWA IEYOSHI (XII)

TOKUGAWA IESADA (XIII)

TOKUGAWA YOSHINOBU (XV)

Handed political power to the emperor intending to get it back, which proved to be a miscalculation...

MUNETAKE

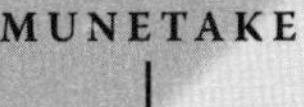

MATSUDAIRA SADANOBU

SENIOR CHAMBERLAIN

TAKIYAMA

Discovered by Masaharu and brought to the Inner Chambers.

TENSHO-IN (TANEATSU)

Iesada's consort, and Iemochi's guardian.

PRINCE KAZU (CHIKAKO)

Iemochi's consort. In fact an imperial princess who came in place of her brother.

TOKUGAWA IESHIGE (IX)

TOKUGAWA IEHARU (X)

SENIOR CHAMBERLAIN

TANUMA OKITSUGU

SENIOR COUNCILLOR

ABE MASAHIRO

GREAT ELDER

II NAOSUKE

TOKUGAWA IEMOCHI (XIV)

Popular shogun who died of illness at age 20.

SENIOR COUNCILLOR

ITAKURA KATSUKIYO

SAIGO TAKAMORI

Samurai from Satsuma and a central figure in the new government.

KATSU KAISHU

Dismissed naval commissioner who retains a strong allegiance to Iemochi.

EMPEROR KOMEI

The previous emperor, who died suddenly, and Prince Kazu's elder brother by another mother.

THE INNER CHAMBERS

Ōoku

THE INNER CHAMBERS

"Resignation of titles and surrender of lands."

This was the demand made by the new government of Tokugawa Yoshinobu—to relinquish not only the post of shogun, but also the court title of minister of the center and to surrender all territories belonging to the Tokugawa shogunate to the emperor.

MY OWN FEELINGS ARE ONE THING, AND THOSE OF THE DIRECT RETAINERS OF THE TOKUGAWA FAMILY ARE ANOTHER. WHAT WILL THEY THINK, GIVEN SUCH AN ORDER...?

AND THAT'S NOT THE ONLY CONSIDERATION. THE AIZU AND KUWANA DOMAINS, WHICH ARE CHARGED WITH GUARDING ME HERE AT NIJO CASTLE, HAVE HEARD OF THE EDICT AND ARE FURIOUS. IF THEY SHOULD ERUPT IN VIOLENT PROTEST, I WOULD NOT BE ABLE TO HOLD THEM BACK ON MY OWN.

FOR THESE REASONS, I REQUEST A DELAY IN THE IMPLEMENTATION OF THE ORDER.

HMPH...THOSE SATSUMA AND CHOSHU BUMPKINS SEEM TO THINK THAT SIMPLY ISSUING AN ORDER TO RESTORE IMPERIAL RULE WILL MAKE POLITICAL POWER DROP INTO THEIR LAPS. LET THEM THINK AGAIN.

I'LL MAKE SURE THEY UNDERSTAND VERY WELL WHERE POLITICAL POWER IN THIS COUNTRY RESTS—IN MY HANDS, AND MINE ALONE!

AND THAT WASN'T ALL... I HEARD THAT LATER, WHEN HE MOVED FROM KYOTO TO OSAKA, HE INVITED MINISTERS FROM BRITAIN, AMERICA, FRANCE, HOLLAND, ITALY, AND PRUSSIA TO OSAKA CASTLE AND MADE BRAZEN PROCLAMATIONS TO EACH ONE IN TURN...

IT MAY APPEAR TO BE A RATHER TUMULTUOUS TIME IN JAPAN, BUT IN FACT THE TOKUGAWA SHOGUNATE FIRMLY RETAINS ITS GRIP ON POWER.

AND I, YOSHINOBU, AM PERSONALLY IN CHARGE OF FOREIGN RELATIONS, SO REST ASSURED THAT YOU HAVE NOTHING TO FEAR!

NOT AGAIN... WHOEVER COMES FACE-TO-FACE WITH YOSHINOBU SEEMS TO BE BAMBOOZLED BY HIS WAY WITH WORDS.

IF WE LET HIM GO ON LIKE THIS, OUR ESTABLISHMENT OF A NEW NATIONAL GOVERNMENT WILL BE MEANINGLESS. SO LONG AS TOKUGAWA YOSHINOBU REMAINS ALIVE, THIS COUNTRY SIMPLY CANNOT BE TRANSFORMED!

AND IF THAT BE SO, HE MUST DIE. YOSHINOBU CANNOT BE ALLOWED TO REMAIN ALIVE!

BRING ME ONE OF OUR SECRET AGENTS. THERE IS SOMETHING I WANT MASUMITSU AND HIS MEN IN EDO TO DO FOR ME.
SIR!

IN ORDER TO DEPOSE YOSHINOBU, WE MUST FIRST ENTER A SITUATION OF MILITARY CONFLICT WITH THE TOKUGAWA.
AND TO DO THAT, WE'LL STIR UP TROUBLE IN EDO... FOMENT UNREST AND FORCE THEIR HAND—GET THE TOKUGAWA TO START A WAR WITH US.

IT'S COMPLETE CHAOS OUT THERE.

BURGLA-RIES, LOOTING, ARSON...
KATSU, ARE YOU QUITE SURE THAT SATSUMA IS BEHIND ALL OF IT?
YES.

WE KNOW THAT A SATSUMA RETAINER BY THE NAME OF MASUMITSU KYUNOSUKE HAS BEEN HIRING UNEMPLOYED LORDLESS SAMURAI AND PAYING THEM TO WREAK HAVOC AROUND TOWN. THAT'S AS FAR AS WE'VE GOTTEN.

BUT YOU'RE FAIRLY CERTAIN THAT THE ONE GIVING THIS MASUMITSU HIS ORDERS IS SAIGO TAKAMORI OF SATSUMA, IN KYOTO.

KICHI-NOSUKE...

WHAT SAIGO WANTS MORE THAN ANYTHING RIGHT NOW IS TO OPEN HOSTILITIES WITH THE SHOGUNATE'S ARMY AND CRUSH THE TOKUGAWA ONCE AND FOR ALL THROUGH FORCE. BUT HE DOESN'T WANT TO BE THE ONE WHO STARTS IT. INSTEAD, HE IS TRYING TO GOAD THE SHOGUNATE'S MEN INTO TAKING UP ARMS...
I'M PRETTY SURE LORD YOSHINOBU KNOWS THAT ALL THIS UNREST HERE IN EDO IS BEING FOMENTED BY SATSUMA, AND TO WHAT END. ONE THING HE IS NOT IS STUPID.

HMM... SO THE KEY HERE IS TO WHAT EXTENT LORD YOSHINOBU WILL BE ABLE TO STOP HIS RETAINERS FROM TAKING THE BAIT...
SIR TENSHO-IN!

WHAT'S THE MATTER?!

FIRE, SIR TENSHO-IN! YOU MUST GET AWAY AT ONCE!

WHAT...?

THIS VERY STRUCTURE, THE WESTERN ENCLOSURE, IS ON FIRE, SIR! YOU MUST GET AWAY!

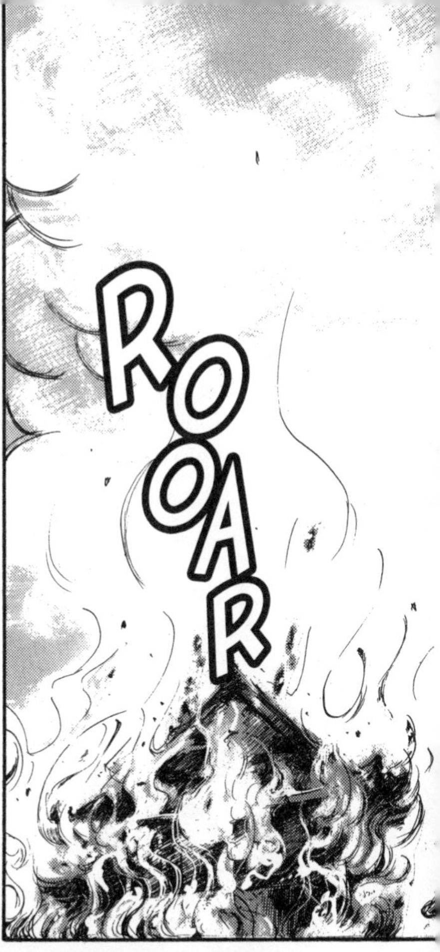
ROAR

NAKA-
ZAWA!
WHERE DID IT START ...?
SIR... IT SEEMS IT WAS NOT THE KITCHENS. SO IT'S CERTAINLY QUITE SUSPICIOUS.

ARSON ...?!

THIS IS CRAZY.
SETTING FIRE TO SIR TENSHO-IN'S RESIDENCE, IN THE HEART OF EDO CASTLE... SATSUMA IS REALLY PUSHING IT...!

TWHOK
GWAGH ...!!
And then, like pouring oil onto that fire, shots were fired into the Edo compound of the Shonai domain, a leading force in the shogunate.
ARGH... NOW WE HAVE CASUALTIES, INCLUDING SOME DEAD!
And of course, warriors of the Shonai domain were not going to take that lying down.
WE KNOW THAT SATSUMA WAS BEHIND THIS! LET'S GO DOWN TO THE SATSUMA COMPOUND IN MITA AND BURN IT TO THE GROUND!
YEAH!
News of the Shonai domain's revenge arson attack on the Satsuma domain's Edo compound traveled immediately to Osaka Castle.
LORD YOSHINOBU!! WE CANNOT AFFORD TO WAIT A MOMENT LONGER!!
THEY SHOT AT AND KILLED WARRIORS FROM THE SHONAI DOMAIN! THEY SET FIRE TO THE WESTERN ENCLOSURE OF EDO CASTLE ITSELF! THIS IS BEYOND OUTRAGEOUS!!
SATSUMA MUST BE DESTROYED !!

STRIKING BACK IS EXACTLY WHAT SAIGO WANTS YOU TO DO. DON'T FALL INTO HIS TRAP!
DO WE HAVE YOUR PERMISSION, LORD YOSHINOBU?!
PLEASE DON'T!

YES!
And so it was that the new government's army and the shogunate's army clashed at Toba and Fushimi, just south of Kyoto, in the opening battles of another civil war.
AAAAAAGH ...!
SO HE COULDN'T GRIT HIS TEETH AND WAIT IT OUT...

The leaders of the shogunate continued to be putty in the hands of Saigo Takamori, whose unparalleled ability to envision outcomes had been honed in the pragmatic "if this, then what?" postulation system of "local education" in Satsuma.

BUT, SIR TAKIYAMA! SIR TAKIYAMA! THE TOKUGAWA FORCES FAR OUTNUMBER THE NEW GOVERNMENT'S FORCES, SO THEY'RE SURE TO WIN, AREN'T THEY, SIR?!
HMM...
ACCORDING TO KATSU, THE TOKUGAWA ARMY HAS MORE OR LESS SUCCEEDED IN WESTERNIZING ITSELF.

At this point in the hostilities, the fighting was back and forth, and as Katsu said, the shogunate forces had as good a chance of winning as the other side.
...

DON'T WORRY.
IT'LL BE ALL RIGHT. YES, A NEW GOVERNMENT HAS BEEN DECLARED, BUT THE FACT IS THAT THE TOKUGAWA HAVE NOT RELINQUISHED ANY OF THEIR TERRITORIES, AND LORD YOSHINOBU IS QUITE A STRATEGIST.
EVEN IF WE DO NOT WIN THIS WAR, IF WE CAN COME OUT OF IT WITHOUT LOSING, LORD YOSHINOBU WILL HAVE ROOM TO MANEUVER IN THE SUBSEQUENT NEGOTIATIONS. IT WILL TURN OUT ALL RIGHT.

IF I MIGHT BLOW MY OWN HORN, OUR NAVY IS FAR SUPERIOR TO THEIRS.
EVEN IF THEY ROUTED US ON LAND, ALL WE'D HAVE TO DO IS WAIT FOR THEM TO ADVANCE AS FAR AS THE TOKAIDO HIGHWAY, AND WE WOULD BOMBARD THEM FROM OUR WARSHIPS IN SURUGA BAY!

...
IN ALL HONESTY, DO YOU BELIEVE LORD YOSHINOBU CAN PREVAIL OVER THE NEW GOVERNMENT'S FORCES?
PROBABLY, YES.
AFTER ALL, LORD YOSHINOBU'S A MAN OF QUICK WIT AND SILVER TONGUE. EVEN STRIPPED OF MY POSITION, I WOULDN'T BE THIS EASYGOING ABOUT IT ALL IF I DIDN'T BELIEVE THAT.

CHANGING THE SUBJECT, SIR TAKIYAMA... HAVE YOU ALREADY FINISHED WEBSTER'S SPELLING BOOK?
MM. I'VE MOVED ON TO SARGENT'S SECOND READER.
AND I'VE OBTAINED SOME COPIES OF THE ENGLISH-LANGUAGE NEWSPAPER BEING PUBLISHED IN YOKOHAMA FOR FOREIGN RESIDENTS THERE.

AH, THE *DAILY JAPAN HERALD*! THAT'S A GREAT IDEA! IT'S THE BEST PLACE TO LEARN THE MOST CURRENT, IDIOMATIC ENGLISH. YOU'LL FIND IT A VERY INTERESTING WAY TO CONTINUE YOUR STUDIES.

I CAN UNDERSTAND MOST OF THE MEANING NOW, BUT HOW TO PRONOUNCE THE WORDS ELUDES ME... I'M SELF-TAUGHT, AFTER ALL.

ALL RIGHT, THEN! STARTING TODAY WE'LL PLACE A SPECIAL EMPHASIS ON PRONUNCIATION!

At this juncture, Katsu was still taking an optimistic view of how the Tokugawa would fare in this war.

Because, at this juncture, he still did not know what Saigo Takamori was planning to do next...

HEH HEH... THE PLAN SAIGO HAS COME UP WITH IS A GOOD ONE. FIRST PAY LORDLESS SAMURAI IN EDO TO STIR UP A LOT OF TROUBLE AND CAUSE DISTURBANCES AROUND THE CITY.

Iwakura Tomomi, formerly of the court and now a leading member of the new government, had in fact studied a book entitled *Imperial Flags and Banners* and commissioned certain articles to be made, three months before this war had even broken out.

THEN, WHEN THE TOKUGAWA GET RILED UP AND CALL THEIR SOLDIERS TO OSAKA TO FIGHT THE NEW GOVERNMENT'S FORCES, WE RENAME THEM "THE IMPERIAL ARMY" AND ROUND ON THE TOKUGAWA AS "ENEMIES OF THE COURT."

AND THESE ARE OUR SECRET WEAPON!

FWAP

LISTEN YE! THESE IMPERIAL BROCADE BANNERS ARE NOTHING LESS THAN THE MIKADO'S BATTLE FLAGS!

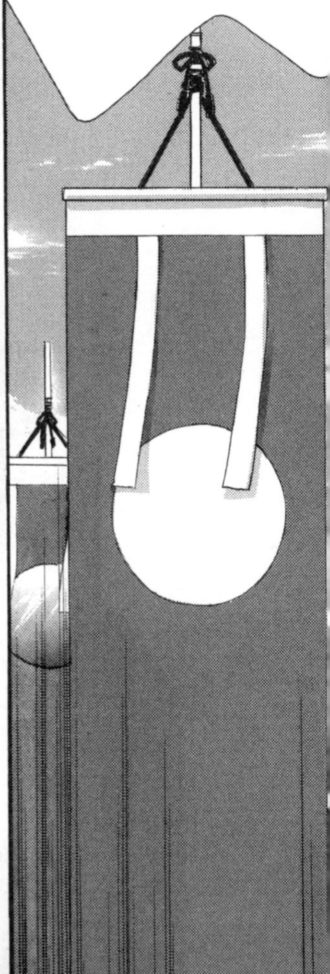

IMPERIAL BROCADE BANNERS ...?!

YEAH...!! I'VE HEARD THEM DESCRIBED BY STORYTELLERS, RECOUNTING THE WAR CHRONICLES OF OLD! RED DAMASK WITH A GOLD BROCADE SUN AND A SILVER BROCADE MOON...!

...

NOW LET US DEFEAT THE TRAITOROUS TOKUGAWA, ENEMIES OF THE EMPEROR! WE HAVE NOTHING TO FEAR!

FOR WE ARE THE MIKADO'S OWN SOLDIERS—THE IMPERIAL ARMY!

LET'S GO!

WOOOOO!

And so it was that on the 11th day of the first month, Katsu came upon a shocking sight.

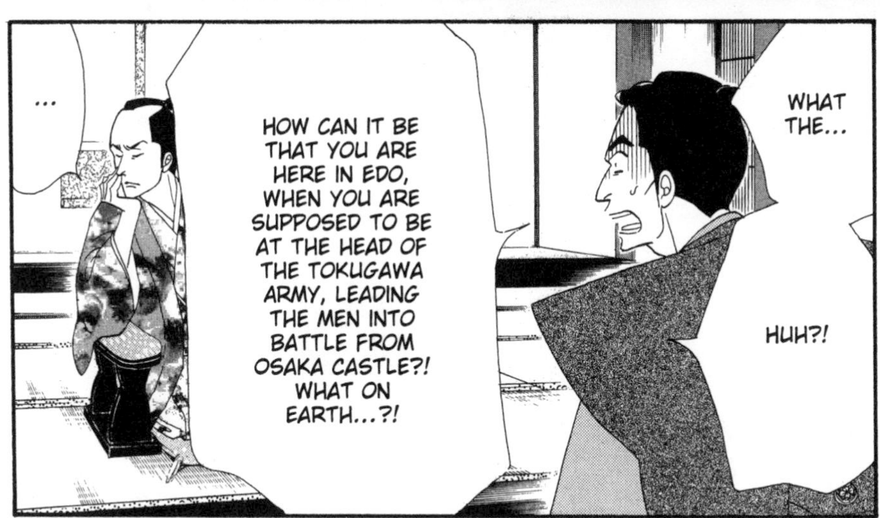
WHAT THE...
HUH?!
HOW CAN IT BE THAT YOU ARE HERE IN EDO, WHEN YOU ARE SUPPOSED TO BE AT THE HEAD OF THE TOKUGAWA ARMY, LEADING THE MEN INTO BATTLE FROM OSAKA CASTLE?! WHAT ON EARTH...?!
...

Upon hearing that the other side had raised the imperial brocade banners as their standards, Yoshinobu had concluded that it was all over for the Tokugawa. Taking just a few close aides, he had crept out of Osaka Castle and returned to Edo aboard the warship *Kaiyo-maru*.

WHAT ...?!

ARE YOU SAYING YOU ABANDONED YOUR SOLDIERS, WHO ARE FIGHTING THE ENEMY IN OSAKA AS WE SPEAK, AND FLED BACK TO EDO—YOU, WHO ARE THEIR COMMANDING GENERAL...?!

THE TRUTH OF THE MATTER IS THAT FIGHTING CONTINUES, AND YOU—WHILE TALKING ABOUT ENDING THIS SENSELESS WAR—HAVE NOT TAKEN ONE STEP TOWARD NEGOTIATING A CEASE-FIRE WITH THE NEW GOVERNMENT, WHICH IS THE ONLY WAY TO END IT!

IF CREEPING OUT OF OSAKA CASTLE IN THE DEAD OF NIGHT TO AVOID DISCOVERY BY YOUR SOLDIERS IS NOT ABANDONING THEM AND FLEEING, THEN WHAT WOULD YOU CALL IT?!

BUT IF I REMAIN THERE AND CONTINUE FIGHTING, THAT MAKES ME AN ENEMY OF THE COURT!

BUT WHAT IF WE LOSE...?!
IF WE LOSE, HISTORY WILL BRAND ME THE LEADER OF A REBEL ARMY, WHEN IN FACT THE MITO BRANCH OF THE TOKUGAWA FAMILY HAS FOR GENERATIONS COMMINGLED SHOGUNAL AND COURTLY BLOOD—WHEN IN FACT, HALF THE BLOOD THAT RUNS THROUGH MY VERY VEINS IS THAT OF THE IMPERIAL FAMILY...!
I COULD NOT BEAR IT! I SIMPLY CANNOT ENDURE THE THOUGHT THAT I, WHO HAIL FROM THE MITO TOKUGAWA, MIGHT BE CALLED A TRAITOROUS ENEMY OF THE COURT...!
ALL HE CARES ABOUT IS HIMSELF, AND NOT A FIG FOR THE LIVES OF THE SOLDIERS. AND NOW HE'S GOING ON ABOUT THE BLOOD IN HIS VEINS?!
IN THAT CASE, WHY DID YOU TAKE UP SATSUMA'S GAUNTLET AND START THIS WAR IN THE FIRST PLACE?! ALL YOU HAD TO DO WAS THINK AGAIN AND NOT GO FORWARD WITH IT!
AT THE TIME, I THOUGHT WE COULD WIN!

THERE ARE FAR MORE URGENT THINGS FOR YOU TO BE DOING RIGHT NOW THAN LINING UP THESE SPECIOUS ARGUMENTS TO GET THE BETTER OF ME.

AT THIS VERY MOMENT, GREAT NUMBERS OF TOKUGAWA ARMY SOLDIERS ARE LOSING THEIR LIVES IN OSAKA! AND THIS IS WHAT I WAS SUMMONED HERE OUT OF HOUSE ARREST FOR?!

I CAN'T EVEN LOOK AT YOU ANYMORE. I'M GOING! GOODBYE!

NOT SO FAST, KATSU!

YOU SHALL BE REINSTATED TO THE POST OF NAVAL COMMISSIONER.
NOT ONLY THAT, IMMEDIATELY AFTERWARDS I SHALL PROMOTE YOU TO THE POST OF COMMANDER GENERAL OF THE ARMY AND ENTRUST YOU WITH THE COMMAND OF ALL THE BRANCHES OF THE TOKUGAWA ARMED FORCES.
OH, AND YOU MENTIONED CEASE-FIRE NEGOTIATIONS WITH SATSUMA. I ENTRUST YOU WITH THOSE ALSO.
WHAT...?! SIR ITAKURA ...!
SORRY, KATSU!

"THE FATE OF THE TOKUGAWA FAMILY IS IN YOUR HANDS...!"

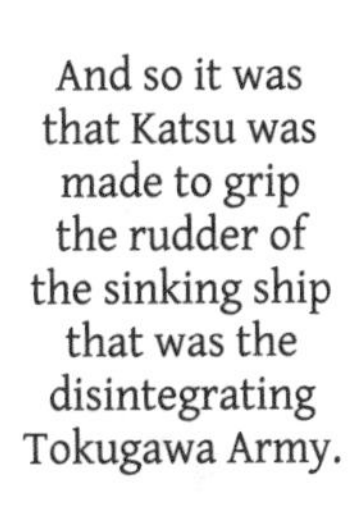

As the shogunate army fell into complete disarray against the new government's self-proclaimed Imperial Army, Yoshinobu paid a visit to Tensho-in in the Inner Chambers, a place he had once so reviled.

SIR TENSHO-IN. I, YOSHINOBU, HAVE COME TO TELL YOU THAT I HAVE JUST RETURNED TO EDO.

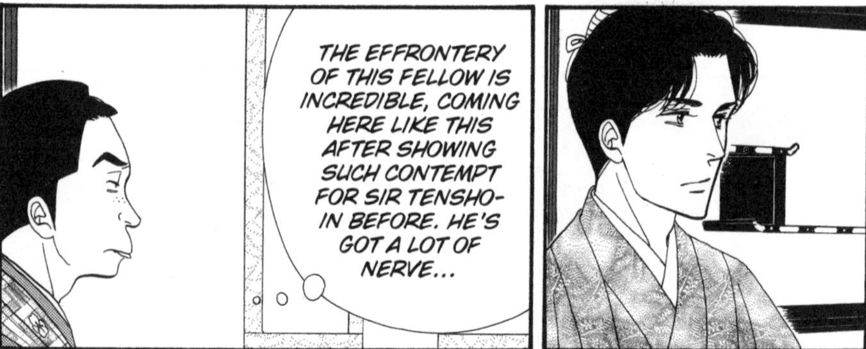

AND?

SIR!

ALTHOUGH I WAS DRAGGED AGAINST MY WILL INTO OPENING HOSTILITIES AGAINST THE SATSUMA-CHOSHU FORCES BY MY FURIOUS VASSALS, WHO REACTED TO SAIGO'S STRATAGEMS EXACTLY AS HE FORESAW, I COULD NOT BEAR BEING TAINTED WITH THE REPREHENSIBLE LABEL "ENEMY OF THE COURT" AND HAVE THEREFORE RETURNED TO EDO.

HOWEVER, IN SPITE OF MY SHOWING THIS DEFERENCE AND INDEED ALLEGIANCE TO THE EMPEROR, THE SATSUMA-CHOSHU ARMY CONTINUES TO PURSUE ME. IT HAS NOW BROKEN THROUGH THE BARRIER AT HAKONE, AND IS HEADING TOWARD EDO TO SACK AND PILLAGE THIS CITY.

FOR THE SAKE OF THE CONTINUATION OF THE TOKUGAWA CLAN, AND IN ORDER TO PREVENT EDO, WHICH IS HOME TO YOU AND PRINCE KAZU, FROM GOING UP IN FLAMES...

...I REQUEST THAT YOU, SIR TENSHO-IN, INTERCEDE WITH SATSUMA—WHICH IS, AFTER ALL, YOUR BIRTHPLACE—TO TO CEASE THIS CAMPAIGN.

Even when begging for his own life, this man managed to make it sound like he was talking about someone else.
SIR TENSHO-IN...
NO !!
WHY SHOULD I HAVE TO MEET YOSHINOBU?! I DON'T WANT TO, AND I WON'T!
IT WAS BECAUSE OF HIM THAT LORD IEMOCHI FELL ILL AND DIED, MORE OR LESS!
LADY CHIKAKO.

AND SHAME ON YOU, SIR TENSHO-IN! TO PROMISE YOU WOULD SEND THE IMPERIAL ARMY GENERALS A LETTER ASKING THEM TO SPARE THAT YOSHINOBU'S LIFE!
I AM NOT DOING IT FOR LORD YOSHINOBU.

IF THE NEW GOVERNMENT'S ARMY SHOULD INVADE EDO IN ORDER TO SLAY LORD YOSHINOBU, THEY WILL SURELY BURN THIS CASTLE AND EVERYTHING AROUND IT TO THE GROUND.
I AM WRITING THAT LETTER NOT TO SAVE LORD YOSHINOBU'S LIFE, BUT TO PREVENT EDO FROM TURNING INTO A SEA OF FLAMES, AND THEN A GRAVEYARD OF ASHES.
I AM DOING IT TO SAVE THE CITY AND THE TOWNSFOLK THAT MEANT SO MUCH TO MY DARLING BELOVED...

MY PRINCE.
IF THE TOKUGAWA FAMILY WERE TO BE DECLARED ENEMIES OF THE EMPEROR AND ABOLISHED, WHAT WOULD HAPPEN TO OUR ADOPTED SON, LORD KAMENOSUKE?

I THINK YOU NOW UNDER-STAND.

SO PLEASE, I BEG YOU TO MEET WITH LORD YOSHINOBU.

STAY HERE WITH ME!
WHEN YOSHINOBU COMES!
IF I'M HERE WITH JUST TSUCHIMIKADO AND NOTO, HE MIGHT FIGURE OUT WE'RE ALL WOMEN IN MY CHAMBERS!
HUH?

Just as Tensho-in had written to his birth family of Shimazu and to Saigo Takamori, Lady Chikako wrote a letter to Hashimoto Saneyana, the commander general of the invading forces, asking him to spare Yoshinobu's life.
But their efforts were in vain... The army led by Saigo Takamori continued its advance towards Edo, where panic and desperation were boiling over in the streets.
EDO IS FINISHED, FOLKS...THEY SAY WHEN THE IMPERIAL ARMY COMES, THEY'LL BURN THE WHOLE CITY DOWN TO THE GROUND!
GET OUT WHILE YOU CAN! TAKE EVERYTHING YOU CAN CARRY, AND GET AS FAR FROM THE CASTLE AS POSSIBLE!

I BEG YOUR PARDON FOR THE SUDDENNESS OF THIS REQUEST, BUT I WOULD LIKE TO RESIGN MY POST.

THERE IS MUCH LOOTING AND VIOLENCE IN THE STREETS, AND MY ELDERLY PARENTS FEEL VERY UNSAFE. THEY ARE TELLING ME TO COME HOME RIGHT AWAY.

Meanwhile, among the men hailing from samurai families, there were those who tendered their resignations for an altogether different reason.

WE SIMPLY CANNOT SIT IDLY BY IN A PLACE LIKE THIS, WHEN MEN ON THE TOKUGAWA SIDE ARE LOSING THEIR LIVES FIGHTING THE SATSUMA-CHOSHU ARMY!

WE WISH TO RESIGN OUR POSTS IMMEDIATELY SO THAT WE MAY JOIN THE TOKUGAWA ARMY STRAIGHTAWAY AND HELP THEM CRUSH THIS SO-CALLED IMPERIAL ARMY!

THAT'S ALL RIGHT, KUROKI. IF WE THINK OF WHAT LIES AHEAD, WE ARE ACTUALLY HELPED BY HAVING PEOPLE COME FORWARD AND ASK TO BE RELIEVED OF THEIR POSTS.

YOU MAY CLOSE OFF ALL THE UNUSED CHAMBERS AND APARTMENTS IF YOU WISH. WITH SUCH FEW STAFF, CLEANING ALL THE WINGS OF THIS ENCLOSURE DAILY IS PROBABLY OUT OF THE QUESTION.

M'LORD ...

SIR TAKI-YAMA.

I'M NOT FROM A SAMURAI FAMILY LIKE THOSE MEN WHO RESIGNED THE OTHER DAY, BUT I CAN HARDLY SIT STILL EITHER! I WANT TO BEAT BACK THE SATSUMA-CHOSHU ARMY WHEN THEY REACH EDO AND HELP VANQUISH THEM!

NAKANO!

Tsk!

HAVE YOU ANY IDEA HOW HARD KATSU IS WORKING, AS COMMANDER GENERAL OF THE ARMY, TO RESTRAIN HOTHEADS LIKE YOU AMONG HIS FORCES?!

LORD YOSHINOBU IS BASICALLY UNDER CONFINEMENT AT KAN'EI-JI TEMPLE, AND THE TOKUGAWA HAVE ALREADY DECLARED ALLEGIANCE TO THE NEW GOVERNMENT. THE TOKUGAWA HAVE LOST!

B-BUT...IF THAT'S SO, WHY DOESN'T THE IMPERIAL ARMY STOP FIGHTING, INSTEAD OF CONTINUING ITS ADVANCE AND THREATENING TO BURN DOWN EDO?!

WHEN THEY GET HERE, THEY'RE GOING TO STORM EDO CASTLE, AREN'T THEY?! WELL, IF THAT HAPPENS, I'M A PROUD SON OF EDO, BORN AND RAISED—AND YOU MAY BE SURE I WILL FIGHT TO DEFEND MY HOME!

OH! TO CHANGE THE SUBJECT SOMEWHAT... SHOULD I SHAVE MY CROWN SOON? I'M REACHING THE AGE...

AND IT SEEMS WRONG THAT I SHOULD KEEP MY FORELOCKS WHEN THE TOKUGAWA ARE FACING SUCH A TERRIBLE CRISIS...

!!

NO, YOU MAY NOT SHAVE YOUR CROWN!! HOW DARE YOU EVEN MENTION IT?!

NOT ONLY DO WE NO LONGER HAVE A LADY SHOGUN TO SERVE, WE CAN'T EVEN LOOK FORWARD TO HIRING ANY NEW VALETS OF THE CHAMBER! IF YOU CUT OFF YOUR FORELOCKS, THIS PLACE WILL BE BEREFT OF ANY KIND OF CHARM OR LOVELINESS AT ALL!

EXACTLY AS HE SAYS! YOU ARE WOEFULLY IGNORANT OF THE IMPORTANCE OF A VALET'S FORELOCKS!

IF YOU CUT YOURS OFF, WE'RE LEFT WITH NOTHING ENDEARING OR LOVABLE IN THESE INNER CHAMBERS BUT CATS!

YES ...
WE WON'T BE HERE FOR MUCH LONGER ...

OH, THAT'S RIGHT. THAT LITTLE SPANIEL BELONGING TO SASAZUKA, THE USHER OF THE PURSE, WHICH WENT MISSING A FEW DAYS AGO...
OH! YOU MUST MEAN PRINCESS SAKURA! SHE'S THE APPLE OF SIR SASAZUKA'S EYE— HE ABSOLUTELY ADORES THAT LITTLE DOG.
Has she been found ?!

LIKE I'M TRYING TO TELL YOU— WORDS LIKE "SUICIDE" AND "WAR" SHOULD NOT BE BANDIED ABOUT WILLY-NILLY!
LISTEN UP! THE ONLY REASON I, OF ALL PEOPLE, TOOK ON THIS POST OF COMMANDING GENERAL OF THE ARMY IS BECAUSE I WANT TO AVERT A FUTILE CIVIL WAR!

WELL, WHEN THEY FINALLY FOUND HER, SHE HAD MULTIPLIED BY FOUR!
OOH! SHE HAD PUPPIES!

IF JAPAN GETS INTO A FULL-SCALE DOMESTIC CONFLICT, WE'LL END UP LIKE CHINA—EUROPE WILL TAKE ADVANTAGE OF THE DISORDER TO COME AND MEDDLE IN OUR INTERNAL POLITICS, AND BEFORE WE KNOW IT, WE'LL BE TURNED INTO A COLONY! THAT IS WHAT I AM TRYING TO AVOID!

HA! I MUST BE ONE OF THE MOST DESPISED COMMANDING GENERALS EVER TO LEAD AN ARMY...

BUT I DON'T CARE! LET THEM CALL ME COWARD AND TRAITOR UNTIL THEIR LUNGS GIVE OUT—I WILL NOT LET THE TOKUGAWA AND IMPERIAL ARMIES GO TO WAR AGAINST EACH OTHER!

BUT FOR THAT, I NEED TO MEET WITH SAIGO AND CHANGE HIS MIND, BEFORE THE IMPERIAL ARMY REACHES EDO...!

No matter that the Tokugawa had indicated they would swear allegiance to the new government—Saigo was determined to launch an all-out attack on Edo and kill Yoshinobu.

WHATEVER ELSE HAPPENS, I HAVE TO CONVINCE SAIGO NOT TO ATTACK EDO!

Ōoku

THE INNER CHAMBERS

Ōoku
THE INNER CHAMBERS

Katsu Kaishu and Saigo Takamori had met once before, in Kyoto four years previously.
At the time, the Tokugawa shogunate and the Satsuma domain were still on the same side in the increasingly divided nation.
THANK YOU FOR TAKING THE TROUBLE TO COME SEE ME TODAY.
I AM KATSU KAISHU, NAVAL COMMISSIONER FOR THE SHOGUNATE.
Saigo had been appointed a commander in the punitive military expedition the shogunate was sending against the Choshu domain for its role in a recent coup attempt in Kyoto.

What sort of man was this naval commissioner Katsu Kaishu, with whom he would be working side by side in this expeditionary force?
AND I AM SAIGO KICHINOSUKE, A RETAINER OF THE SATSUMA DOMAIN. I AM PLEASED TO MAKE YOUR ACQUAINTANCE.
Saigo had requested this meeting, in order to judge the character of this Katsu and at the same time get a sense of how things were inside the shogunate.
AS YOU KNOW, THE EMPEROR HAS ISSUED A PROCLAMATION COMMANDING SATSUMA TO JOIN THE TOKUGAWA SHOGUNATE IN THIS EXPEDITION AGAINST CHOSHU.
AND SO I WOULD LIKE TO INQUIRE OF YOU WHAT THE SHOGUNATE CONSIDERS TO BE ITS PROSPECTS REGARDING THIS EXPEDITION...
HA! HA HA!
PROSPECTS?! WHAT PROSPECTS?! THE SHOGUNATE IS IN SUCH A MESS THAT IT'S HAVING TROUBLE PUTTING THIS EXPEDITIONARY FORCE TOGETHER IN THE FIRST PLACE!

WHAT DO YOU MEAN, THEY'RE HAVING TROUBLE PUTTING THE FORCE TOGETHER ...?
BASICALLY, NONE OF THE SENIOR COUNCILLORS WANT TO TAKE ANY RESPONSIBILITY FOR ANYTHING, SO THERE ISN'T A SINGLE PERSON ABLE OR WILLING TO MAKE A FIRM DECISION!
BUT AT THE SAME TIME, IF ONE OF THEM DOES ADVANCE A SOUND ARGUMENT, HE'S SHUNNED BY THE REST AS A HERETIC.
!
BUT YOU'RE THE NAVAL COMMISSIONER. DON'T THEY LISTEN TO WHAT YOU HAVE TO SAY?
OF COURSE NOT! MY GREAT-GRANDMOTHER WAS A MONEYLENDER, YOU SEE. SHE USED HER PROFITS TO BUY HER WAY INTO THE SAMURAI CLASS—THE LOWEST RANK, OF COURSE.
OBVIOUSLY WE CAN'T EVEN COMPARE TO THOSE OF OUR OWN LEVEL WHO'VE SERVED THE TOKUGAWA FAMILY SINCE THE BATTLE OF SEKIGAHARA IN 1600. I MIGHT HAVE THE POST OF NAVAL COMMISSIONER, BUT MY FAMILY'S SALARY REMAINS JUST 100 HYO OF RICE A YEAR. BACK IN THE OLD DAYS, PEOPLE OF MY RANK WEREN'T EVEN ALLOWED TO OPEN THEIR MOUTHS INSIDE THE CASTLE.

FOR THE SHOGUN'S COUNCILLORS, PEOPLE LIKE ME ARE JUST USEFUL PAWNS THEY CAN TOSS AWAY WHEN THEY'VE SERVED THEIR PURPOSE. WHEN THE SHOGUNATE SUFFERS A SETBACK, THEY RAISE ME UP TO A LOFTY POST TO CLEAN UP THEIR MESS, AND WHEN THAT'S DONE AND I'M JUST A THORN IN THEIR SIDE, THEY DISMISS ME.
SIR KATSU...
SIR SAIGO.
TO TELL YOU THE TRUTH, I DON'T HAVE THE SLIGHTEST INTEREST IN HOW WE GO ABOUT DEFEATING CHOSHU. MILITARY STRATEGY ISN'T MY CONCERN.
WHAT?!
BECAUSE SOMETHING ELSE CONCERNS ME FAR MORE! DON'T YOU AGREE THAT WHAT WE REALLY OUGHT TO BE THINKING ABOUT IS HOW TO SET THIS COUNTRY ON THE RIGHT COURSE IN THE WORLD TODAY?!

THAT'S WHAT I AM FOCUSED ON! IT'S ALL I THINK ABOUT! WE NEED TO GET THIS COUNTRY GOVERNED BY A GROUP OF SMART, CAPABLE PEOPLE AS SOON AS POSSIBLE, RAISE AND TRAIN A MILITARY THAT CAN FIGHT AGAINST THE ARMIES OF THE FOREIGN POWERS, AND SIGN TREATIES WITH THOSE FOREIGN POWERS ON EQUAL TERMS!
THAT'S WHAT I'VE BEEN SAYING ALL ALONG! IF WE DO THOSE THINGS, JAPAN CAN OPEN ITSELF TO TRADE WITHOUT BECOMING A VASSAL OF THE BIG FOREIGN POWERS! I'VE BEEN SAYING IT OVER AND OVER, BUT DOES ANYBODY LISTEN TO ME...?!
WHY DOESN'T ANYBODY THINK OF THE COUNTRY AS A WHOLE? WHY CAN'T THEY SEE BEYOND THEIR OWN CLAN OR THEIR OWN DOMAIN?! IF ALL WE DO IS BICKER AMONG OURSELVES, WE'RE JUST GOING TO END UP AS SOME OTHER COUNTRY'S COLONY!

UH...
OF COURSE... IT'S EXACTLY AS YOU SAY. AND THOUGH I SAY THAT NOW, I MYSELF HAVE BEEN THINKING ONLY IN TERMS OF SATSUMA AND CHOSHU, SATSUMA AND THE SHOGUNATE... I HAVE NEVER GIVEN A THOUGHT TO ANYTHING OUTSIDE THIS COUNTRY...
I HAVE NEVER...
BUT THIS MAN... IN SPITE OF BEING A MINISTER IN THE SHOGUNATE, HIS OUTLOOK EXTENDS FAR BEYOND THE TOKUGAWA. HE'S THINKING OF HOW THIS COUNTRY OUGHT TO FACE THE OUTSIDE WORLD AND ENGAGE WITH IT...!
OH...! PLEASE PARDON MY OUTBURST!
THE TRUTH IS THAT RIGHT NOW I'VE INCURRED THE DISPLEASURE OF THE GRANDEES AND AM ON THE BRINK OF GETTING THE SACK...SO I LET MY RESENTMENT OF THE BIGWIGS GET THE BETTER OF ME! I HOPE YOU'LL FORGET EVERYTHING I JUST SAID!
Damn! I'm going to be fired if I keep this up!
NO! I WILL NEVER FORGET THE WORDS YOU SPOKE TODAY! THEY HAVE MADE A DEEP IMPRESSION UPON ME, SIR...!

...
BUT IF YOU WOULD, SIR KATSU...
WHY IS IT THAT, KNOWING HOW ROTTEN TO THE CORE THE SHOGUNATE IS, YOU REMAIN WITHIN IT? WHY ARE YOU STILL SERVING THE TOKUGAWA?
LET ME ASK YOU IN RETURN, SIR SAIGO. WHY ARE YOU STILL SERVING THE SATSUMA DOMAIN?
AFTER ALL, LORD SHIMAZU NARIAKIRA, TO WHOM YOU DEDICATED YOUR LIFE, IS LONG DEAD. SO WHY DO YOU REMAIN?

...!!
T-TOUCHÉ, SIR...
HA HA... WE SAMURAI ARE A STRAITENED LOT.
AND IN MY CASE, MY DISGUST WITH THE SHOGUNATE'S MINISTERS ASIDE, I AM QUITE BESOTTED WITH THE PRESENT SHOGUN HERSELF. SO WHAT CAN I DO?
SIR SAIGO.
I HAVE ONE DISCIPLE WHO HAS FREED HIMSELF UTTERLY FROM THE CONSTRAINTS OF THE SAMURAI SPIRIT.
I EXPECT HE'LL BE PAYING YOU A VISIT EVENTUALLY... IF AND WHEN HE DOES, I HOPE YOU'LL LISTEN TO WHAT HE HAS TO SAY.
WELL, THEN!

And now, four years later, the two were about to meet again, this time to broker a cease-fire. Saigo was the commander of the new government's army, while Katsu was the commander in chief of the defeated side.

SO YOU GOT YOUR WISH... TO MEET WITH SAIGO FOR FACE-TO-FACE NEGOTIATIONS...!

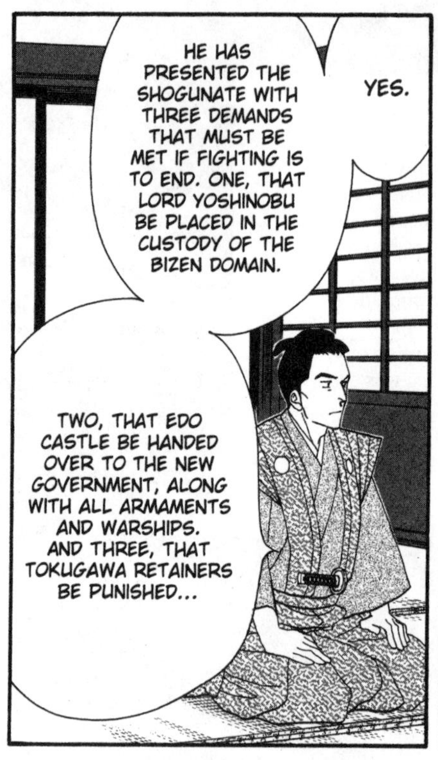
YES.
HE HAS PRESENTED THE SHOGUNATE WITH THREE DEMANDS THAT MUST BE MET IF FIGHTING IS TO END. ONE, THAT LORD YOSHINOBU BE PLACED IN THE CUSTODY OF THE BIZEN DOMAIN.
TWO, THAT EDO CASTLE BE HANDED OVER TO THE NEW GOVERNMENT, ALONG WITH ALL ARMAMENTS AND WARSHIPS. AND THREE, THAT TOKUGAWA RETAINERS BE PUNISHED...

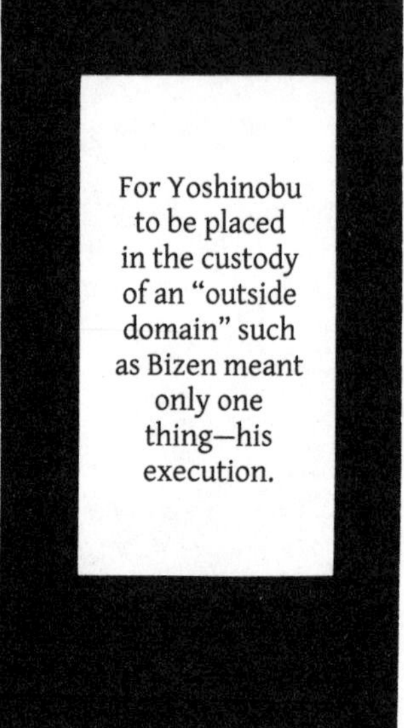
For Yoshinobu to be placed in the custody of an "outside domain" such as Bizen meant only one thing—his execution.

I SEE.
THEY MEAN TO KILL LORD YOSHINOBU AND UTTERLY DESTROY THE TOKUGAWA CLAN.
BUT IF THE SHOGUNATE DOES NOT AGREE TO THESE DEMANDS, SAIGO WILL PROCEED WITH A FULL-SCALE ASSAULT ON EDO, IS THAT RIGHT?

IT'S PREPOSTEROUS TO THINK THE TOKUGAWA WOULD ACCEPT THOSE CONDITIONS!
TO HAVE THAT ILLUSTRIOUS NAME AND LINEAGE EXTINGUISHED, THEIR LORD PUT TO DEATH... THE TOKUGAWA VASSALS WON'T STAND FOR IT. THIS WILL LEAD TO A FULL-BLOWN CIVIL WAR, THERE'S NO DOUBT ABOUT THAT. THERE WILL BE FIGHTING THROUGHOUT THE COUNTRY.
AND THAT WOULD GIVE FOREIGN POWERS AN OPENING TO MEDDLE IN OUR INTERNAL AFFAIRS...
BUT, KATSU...
AT THE MOMENT, BOTH THE NEW GOVERNMENT'S ARMY AND OUR SIDE ARE WAVING THEIR FISTS IN THE AIR, WITH NO IDEA HOW TO BRING THEM DOWN.
I THINK IT MIGHT BE DIFFICULT TO CHANGE SAIGO'S MIND SIMPLY BY MEETING WITH HIM.

WHAT...?!

I'VE BEEN A FIREMAN FOR DECADES NOW, MASTER KATSU, AND I'VE PUT MY LIFE ON THE LINE TIME AND AGAIN, PUTTING FIRES OUT ALL OVER TOWN.

NOW YOU'RE TELLING US—THE FELLAS WHO PUT THE FIRES OUT—TO LIGHT FIRES THROUGHOUT THE CITY...?!

IF WE BURN EDO DOWN OURSELVES BEFORE THE NEW GOVERNMENT'S ARMY ENTERS THE CITY, THEY'LL HAVE NO REASON TO ATTACK ANYMORE!

LOOK, TATSUGORO. YOU FIREMEN KNOW HOW TO READ THE WIND. YOU CAN TELL FROM HOW THE WIND IS BLOWING WHERE TO LIGHT FIRES SO THEY WILL SPREAD ACROSS THE ENTIRE CITY!

THAT'S EXACTLY RIGHT!

LEAVE IT TO US!

AND YOU BOYS FROM THE FISH MARKET, YOU'RE IN CHARGE OF PROTECTING THE FLEEING TOWNSPEOPLE, ALL RIGHT?!

HA HA HA HA
SURE THING, SIR!
US FISHMONGERS GOT SHARP KNIVES, AND WE KNOW HOW TO USE 'EM. WE'LL GUT THOSE SATSUMA BUMPKINS AND FILLET THEM!

ALL OF YOU! LET'S SHOW THOSE NEW GOVERNMENT SOLDIERS WHAT KIND OF METTLE WE SONS OF EDO HAVE!
BUT LET ME BE ABSOLUTELY CLEAR—THIS SCORCHED-EARTH TACTIC IS OUR FINAL TRUMP CARD, THE VERY LAST ACE UP OUR SLEEVE. DO NOT MAKE A MOVE UNTIL I GIVE THE SIGNAL!

...

IT GOES WITHOUT SAYING THAT THIS IS ALSO A BLUFF.

SAIGO AND HIS ARMY OUGHT TO KNOW THAT THE TOKUGAWA'S MOST VALUABLE ASSET IS NOT ITS TERRITORIES—THOUGH THEIR WORTH IS FOUR MILLION KOKU—IT'S THIS CITY OF EDO, WITH ITS MORE THAN ONE MILLION INHABITANTS.
EDO IS ONE OF THE GREAT CITIES OF THE WORLD, ON A PAR WITH LONDON AND PARIS.
IF EDO BURNS DOWN, THE TRADING PORT OF YOKOHAMA JUST SOUTH OF HERE WILL COME TO A COMPLETE STOP. AND THEN BRITAIN, WHICH WAS REAPING SO MUCH PROFIT FROM ITS EXPORT OF RAW SILK FROM JAPAN, WILL INCUR HUGE LOSSES...

BRITAIN, AS YOU KNOW, IS A POWERFUL FRIEND AND SUPPORTER OF SATSUMA.
I DIDN'T TELL THE TOWNSPEOPLE I ENTRUSTED WITH THE SCORCHED-EARTH SCHEME TO KEEP THE PLAN A SECRET. I FULLY EXPECT WORD OF IT TO REACH THE EARS OF THE BRITISH LEGATION AND AM CERTAIN THEY WILL PREVAIL UPON SAIGO TO CALL OFF HIS INVASION. THE ENTIRE PLAN IS A BLUFF!
AND I AM COUNTING ON IT TO WORK!
AND SO, THAT IS THE PLAN. IT REMAINS TO BE SEEN HOW IT PLAYS OUT.
BUT, AT THE VERY LEAST, I GUARANTEE THAT THE TOKUGAWA ARMY WILL NEVER TAKE YOU OR PRINCE KAZU AS HOSTAGES TO USE IN NEGOTIATIONS WITH THE OTHER SIDE. I SWEAR THAT UPON MY HONOR.
KATSU !!

ARE YOU GOING ALONE TO PARLEY WITH SAIGO?!

NO, I PLAN TO TAKE TWO OR THREE OTHERS WITH ME. WHY, SIR?
THEN LET ME BE ONE OF THEM! TAKE ME WITH YOU, KATSU!

I'VE MET SAIGO BEFORE!
THAT MIGHT BE SOMETHING! IT JUST MIGHT SERVE AS A TINY OPENING TO MAKE SOMETHING SHIFT INSIDE HIM!

GLINT
VERY GOOD!
HAVING SIR TENSHO-IN AS PART OF OUR DELEGATION—I SHALL USE THAT TO OUR ADVANTAGE, CERTAINLY!
YES, LET US GO TOGETHER!

I'LL GO TOO!!

OH, UH...ACTUALLY, IT WOULD BE QUITE ENOUGH IF YOU COULD LEND ME THE LETTER, WRITTEN IN THE PREVIOUS EMPEROR'S OWN HAND, THAT LORD IEMOCHI SECURED FOR YOU...

NO! I'LL GO TOO!!

...

IF YOU REFUSE TO LET ME ACCOMPANY YOU AND KATSU, SIR TENSHO-IN, I WILL TAKE THAT LETTER THAT'S IN MY POSSESSION AND BURN IT! DO YOU UNDERSTAND?!

WHAT?!
SAIGO OF SATSUMA IS PLANNING TO ATTACK EDO ON THE 15TH OF MARCH?!

YES, SIR.
AND IT SEEMS THE TOKUGAWA INTEND TO THWART THIS ATTACK BY EMPLOYING THE SCORCHED-EARTH TACTIC THE RUSSIANS USED AGAINST NAPOLEON. THEY PLAN TO BURN EDO DOWN THEMSELVES, BEFORE SAIGO CAN.

IF WE LEAVE MATTERS AS THEY STAND, EDO WILL BE A SEA OF FLAMES, REGARDLESS OF WHICH WAY THE WIND BLOWS...
WE CANNOT HAVE IT!
THERE IS NO ADVANTAGE FOR US WHATSOEVER IN BEING FRIENDLY WITH THE NEW GOVERNMENT IF EDO IS A SMOKING RUIN—WHAT WOULD BE LEFT FOR US TO TRADE?!

SATOW! SEND AN ENVOY TO SAIGO OF SATSUMA AT ONCE!

And so...
COMMANDER SAIGO, SIR! A MEMORANDUM HAS JUST ARRIVED FROM SIR PARKES, THE BRITISH MINISTER!

"THE TOKUGAWA HAVE PLEDGED THEIR ALLEGIANCE TO THE NEW GOVERNMENT.
ATTACKING A FOE WHO HAS ALREADY SURRENDERED TO YOU, AND FURTHERMORE EXECUTING YOSHINOBU, YOUR FOE'S LORD, WOULD BE IN CONTRAVENTION OF INTER-NATIONAL LAW," HE SAYS.

SIR SAIGO! WHAT IS THIS MEMORANDUM TO US?! THIS SIR PARKES MAY BE A BRITISH BIGWIG, BUT THIS IS JAPAN—WE'VE GOT OUR OWN WAY OF DOING THINGS!
EXACTLY RIGHT! WE DON'T NEED TO LISTEN TO WHAT A BRITISH LORD SAYS!
...

IF I PAY NO HEED TO INTERNATIONAL LAW AND GO FORWARD WITH THE ATTACK ON EDO, THE WESTERN POWERS MAY VIEW JAPAN AS A BARBARIC AND BACKWARD NATION, AND POUR SCORN ON US. THAT WOULD NOT BE GOOD.
BUT!
...

CHRP
CHRP
CHRP

WELL.
SHALL WE BE ON OUR WAY?

NAKAMURA AND SUGITA. YOU STAY HERE, IN THIS ROOM.

DON'T SHOW YOURSELVES UNLESS I CALL YOU.

SIR!

IT WILL BE DIFFICULT TO CARRY OUT NEGOTIATIONS WITH SIR SAIGO IF HE KNOWS FROM THE OUTSET THAT SIR TENSHO-IN IS HERE. I BEG YOU, SIR TENSHO-IN, TO WAIT HERE IN THE ADJOINING ROOM FOR THE TIME BEING.

FOR NOW, I ASK ONLY SIR TAKIYAMA TO JOIN ME.

IT HAS BEEN A FEW YEARS.
INDEED, IT HAS BEEN A LONG TIME.

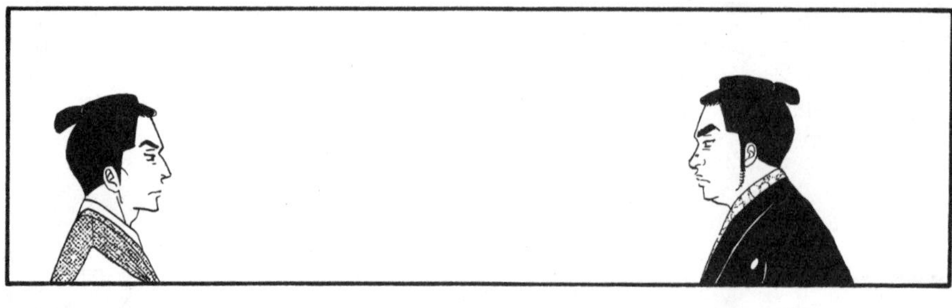

AND YOU ARE NOW THE COMMANDER IN CHIEF OF THE SHOGUNATE'S ARMED FORCES, AT THE HELM OF BOTH THE ARMY AND THE NAVY.
HA HA! YES, AND MY SALARY REMAINS EXACTLY WHAT IT WAS THE LAST TIME WE SPOKE—100 HYO OF RICE A YEAR. WHAT GREAT SUCCESS I'VE ACHIEVED, EH?!

SO THIS IS THE SAIGO TAKAMORI I'VE BEEN HEARING SO MUCH ABOUT...
SIR KATSU.

...IT WAS A REAL SHAME, WHAT HAPPENED TO SIR SAKAMOTO.

IT CERTAINLY WAS.
IF HE WERE STILL ALIVE, IT COULD WELL BE THAT EVERYTHING WOULD HAVE COME TOGETHER, AND YOU AND I WOULDN'T EVEN NEED TO BE HERE FOR THIS PARLEY.

I'M NOT SO SURE ABOUT THAT. EVEN IF HE WERE STILL HERE, I DON'T BELIEVE MY VIEWS WOULD BE ANY DIFFERENT.
SIMPLY PUT, THE TOKUGAWA ARE AN IMPEDIMENT TO THE COUNTRY THE NEW GOVERNMENT IS TRYING TO BUILD.

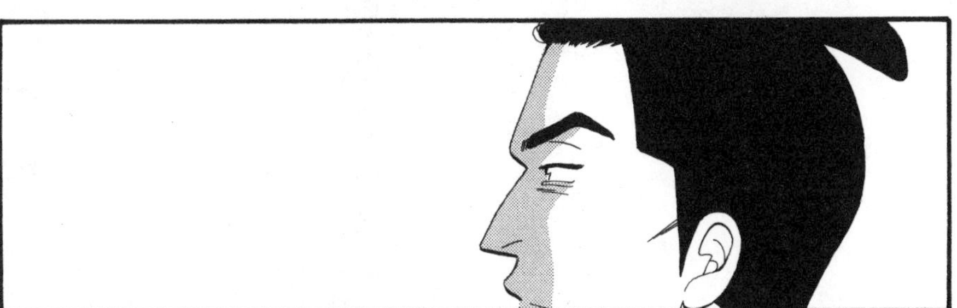

REGARDLESS, YOU'RE SAYING THAT UNLESS WE AGREE TO THE THREE CONDITIONS YOU PUT FORWARD, YOUR FORCES WILL CARRY OUT AN ALL-OUT ATTACK ON EDO.

HMMMM.

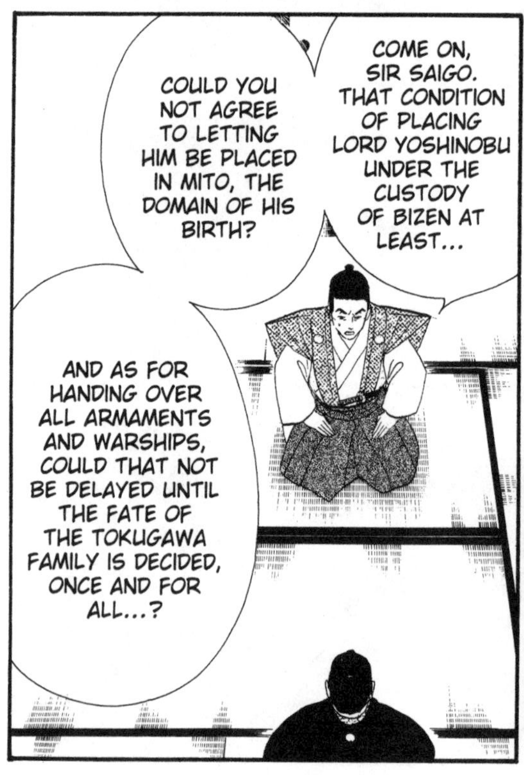

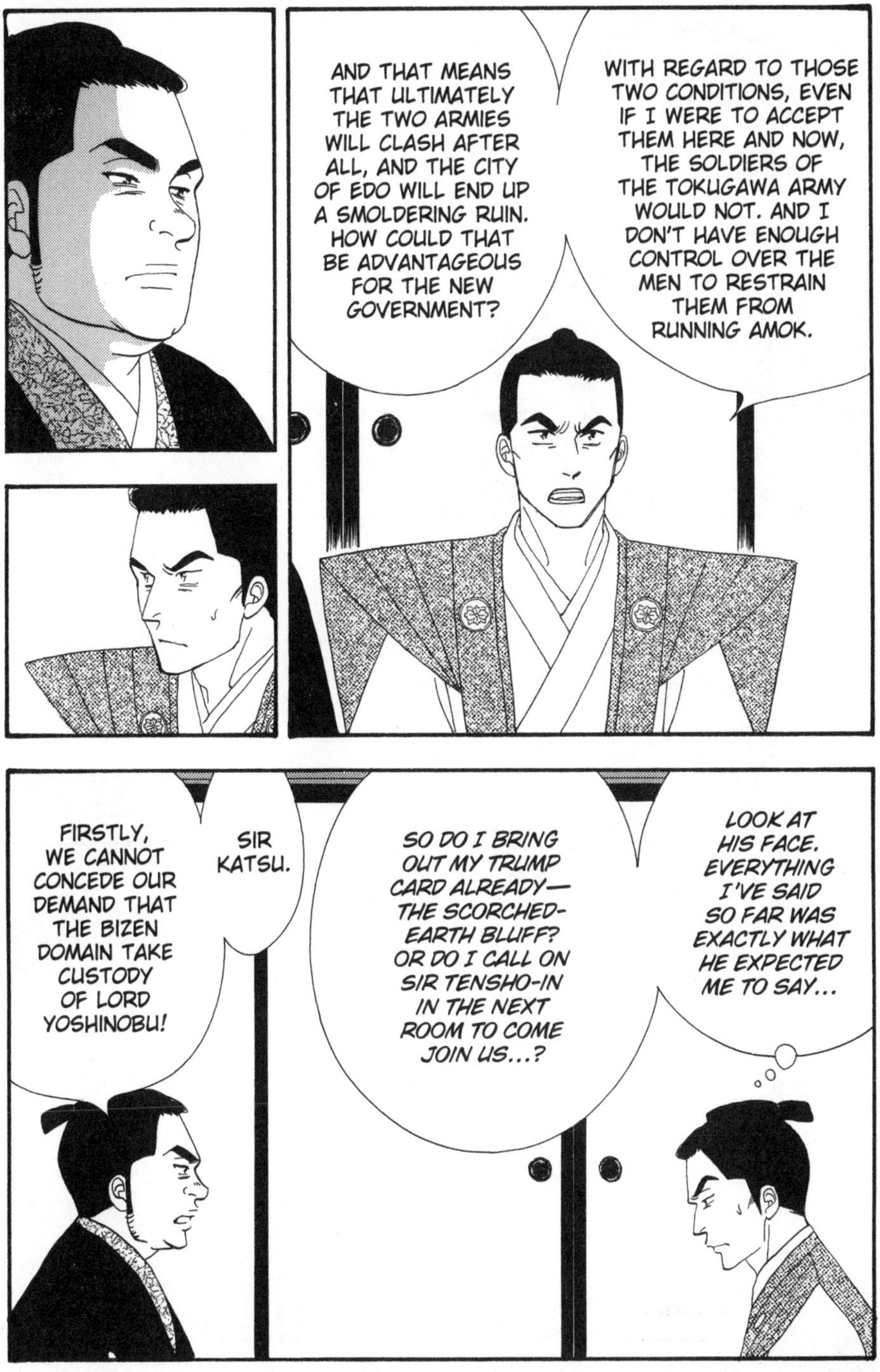

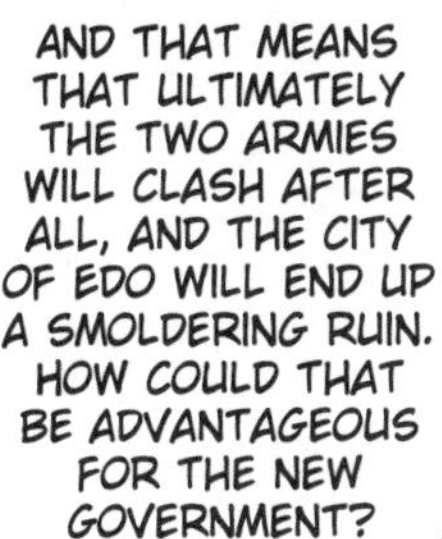

LOOK AT HIS FACE. EVERYTHING I'VE SAID SO FAR WAS EXACTLY WHAT HE EXPECTED ME TO SAY...

SO DO I BRING OUT MY TRUMP CARD ALREADY— THE SCORCHED-EARTH BLUFF? OR DO I CALL ON SIR TENSHO-IN IN THE NEXT ROOM TO COME JOIN US...?

SIR KATSU.

FIRSTLY, WE CANNOT CONCEDE OUR DEMAND THAT THE BIZEN DOMAIN TAKE CUSTODY OF LORD YOSHINOBU!

REST ASSURED, HOWEVER, THAT BIZEN WILL NOT EXECUTE LORD YOSHINOBU, IF THAT IS WHAT YOU FEAR.

I WILL MAKE SURE THEY PROVIDE THE PROPER CONDITIONS FOR HIM TO PERFORM SEPPUKU WITH DIGNITY. THAT WAY LORD YOSHINOBU WILL RETAIN HIS HONOR TO THE END.

...!!

LORD YOSHINOBU AS DONE ENOUGH HARM TO THIS COUNTRY TO ERIT THAT PUNISHMENT. E HAS DECEIVED PEOPLE IME AND AGAIN WITH HIS FLUENCY AND RHETORIC, ND BROKEN NUMEROUS PLEDGES HE MADE TO US AND OTHERS.

AND HE HAS AN ADDITIONAL GRAVE CRIME TO ANSWER FOR.

IF THE MAN COMMITS SUICIDE, WE CAN ASSERT THERE WAS NO CONTRAVENTION OF INTER-NATIONAL LAW!

AND THAT IS THIS— HE IS THE HEAD OF THE TOKUGAWA FAMILY, WHICH WAS RESPONSIBLE FOR THIS COUNTRY BEING GOVERNED FOR GENERATIONS BY WOMEN, WHO CLOSED THE COUNTRY OFF FROM THE WORLD AND FROM ALL THE SCIENTIFIC AND TECHNOLOGICAL ADVANCES TO BE FOUND THERE, RESULTING IN JAPAN FALLING SHAMEFULLY BEHIND THE COUNTRIES OF THE WEST!

LOOK AROUND THE WORLD— NEARLY ALL THE POWERFUL NATIONS OF EUROPE AND THE UNITED STATES, WHICH ARE FAR MORE ADVANCED THAN OUR COUNTRY, ARE LED BY MEN.

GREAT BRITAIN HAS A WOMAN, QUEEN VICTORIA, AS ITS HEAD OF STATE, BUT THERE IS NOT ONE WOMAN AMONG HER ADVISERS! IN OTHER WORDS, THE ACTUAL GOVERNANCE OF THE COUNTRY IS BEING CARRIED OUT BY MEN!

OUR COUNTRY WAS LED FOR TWO CENTURIES BY WOMEN WHO HAD NO APTITUDE FOR GOVERNMENT. IT WOULD BE ONE THING IF IT HAD BEEN JUST THE SHOGUN, BUT ALL THE SENIOR COUNCILLORS AND OTHER GOVERNMENT OFFICIALS WERE WOMEN AS WELL.

I UNDERSTAND THAT A PLAGUE DECIMATED THE MALE POPULATION OF JAPAN 200 YEARS AGO, AND THERE WAS NO CHOICE BUT TO LET A WOMAN BE SHOGUN UNTIL A MALE HEIR COULD TAKE HER PLACE. BUT WHAT JUSTIFICATION IS THERE FOR THE 14TH TOKUGAWA SHOGUN BEING A WOMAN, JUST A YEAR OR TWO AGO?! THAT IS WHY THIS COUNTRY IS WEAK, ROTTEN, AND LAGGING BEHIND!

SIR SAIGO! BUT THE PRESENT HEAD OF THE TOKUGAWA FAMILY IS LORD YOSHINOBU, AND HE IS A MAN!

SO WHAT?! PUTTING ONE OR TWO MEN IN THE SHOGUN'S SEAT AT THIS STAGE DOES NOT ERASE TWO CENTURIES OF GOVERNANCE WITH FEMALES AT THE HELM!

IF THE WESTERN POWERS EVER FIND OUT THAT JAPAN WAS RULED BY A BUNCH OF WOMEN FOR SO LONG, WE JAPANESE WILL BE THE LAUGHINGSTOCKS OF THE WORLD, DERIDED AS PRIMITIVE SAVAGES!

NO ONE MUST EVER KNOW WE WERE RULED BY WOMEN! AND IN ORDER TO ERASE THIS DISGRACEFUL CHAPTER IN JAPANESE HISTORY, WE HAVE TO OBLITERATE THE TOKUGAWA!

THAT IS WHY LORD TOKUGAWA YOSHINOBU MUST DIE, NO MATTER WHAT!

SHWAP

MY PRINCE, YOU MUSTN'T!
KATSU!
PRINCE KAZU!
HUH?! P-PRINCE KAZU...?!

WHAT ...?
PRINCE KAZU IS HERE...?!
PLEASE, MY PRINCE, I BEG YOU TO RESTRAIN YOURSELF!
NO! LET GO OF ME!
BUT HIS VOICE IS SO...

ARE YOU KATSU KAISHU? WELL, YOU MAY HAVE COME TO THESE NEGOTIATIONS AS THE DEFEATED SIDE, BUT EVEN SO, HOW CAN YOU SIT THERE AND LET HIM INSULT OUR LORD LIKE THAT, AND SAY NOTHING IN RETURN?!
LORD IEMOCHI SPOKE OF YOU OFTEN, KATSU KAISHU! SHE HAD HIGH HOPES FOR YOU AND TOOK YOU UNDER HER WING— AS YOU WELL KNOW. AND YET YOU, THE RECIPIENT OF HER GENEROUS PATRONAGE, SEEM TO HAVE TAKEN A VOW OF SILENCE WHILE OUR LORD IS SLANDERED BY THIS FELLOW!
HE'S A WOMAN?!

MY PRINCE! THE LETTERS!

!!

S-SIR TANEATSU ...?!

YES, KICHINOSUKE! IT'S BEEN A GREAT MANY YEARS SINCE WE LAST SAW EACH OTHER, BUT UNFORTUNATELY NOW IS NOT THE TIME FOR FOND REMINISCENCES!

U-UH, SIR TAKIYAMA. HOW CAN IT BE THAT THIS PERSON HERE IS PRINCE KAZU...?!

IT'S A LONG STORY, SO I'LL TELL IT TO YOU LATER!

KICHINOSUKE. NAY, SAIGO TAKAMORI. READ THESE LETTERS WITH GREAT CARE.
THEY WERE WRITTEN BY THE AUGUST HAND OF THE PREVIOUS MIKADO, HIS MAJESTY EMPEROR KOMEI!
WHAT THE HELL IS GOING ON IN THERE?!
THAT WAS A WOMAN'S VOICE JUST NOW!
BUT SIR SAIGO WAS CLEAR THAT WE'RE NOT TO ENTER UNTIL HE CALLS US...!

CHRRS
CHRRS
CHRRS
CHRRS
CHRRS
CHRRS
TWEET
TWEET
TWEET

...

UMM... MAY I HAVE A LOOK AT THOSE LATER? THEY MIGHT AFFECT OUR NEGOTIATIONS...
YES, OF COURSE!

PHLAP

...

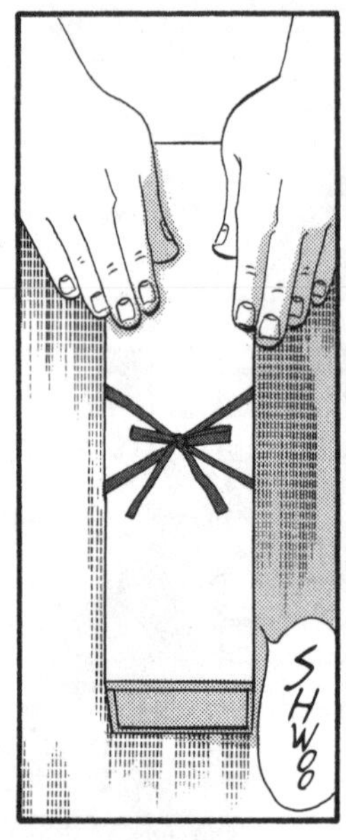
SHWOO

SAIGO.
INDEED I AM A WOMAN. AS IT IS WRITTEN IN THE FIRST LETTER YOU JUST READ, MY YOUNGER BROTHER, PRINCE KAZU, SUDDENLY HID HIMSELF OUT OF SIGHT JUST BEFORE HIS DEPARTURE FOR EDO. I CAME HERE IN HIS STEAD.

AND I THINK IT IS WORTH NOTING THAT A MEMBER OF YOUR NEW GOVERNMENT, IWAKURA TOMOMI, NOT ONLY KNEW ABOUT THIS SCHEME TO PASS ME OFF AS MY BROTHER, BUT WAS EVEN INVOLVED IN IT. HM?

IWAKURA SENT ME OFF TO EDO KNOWING FULL WELL THAT I WAS AN ABSOLUTE IMPOSTER—A CHANGELING, IF YOU WILL. THAT FACT ALONE SPEAKS VOLUMES ABOUT WHAT A SLY, DUPLICITOUS PLOTTER THAT IWAKURA IS!

BUT HIS FAR GREATER CRIME, MORE HEINOUS AND UNSPEAKABLE BY FAR, WAS WHAT YOU READ IN THE OTHER LETTER—HIS POISONING OF EMPEROR KOMEI!

"THE PLOTTERS ARE IWAKURA AND SATSUMA"!

"THE PLOTTERS ARE IWAKURA AND SATSUMA"... IT NO LONGER MATTERS IF YOU YOURSELF WERE INVOLVED IN THAT PLOT OR TO WHAT EXTENT.
BUT IF THE NEW GOVERNMENT AND ITS ARMY ARE NOW GOING TO FORCE IMPOSSIBLE DEMANDS ON THE TOKUGAWA AND THREATEN TO PLUNGE THE CITY OF EDO INTO WAR IF THOSE DEMANDS ARE NOT MET, THEN I WILL MAKE THE CONTENTS OF BOTH OF THOSE LETTERS PUBLIC. DO YOU UNDERSTAND ME?!
WHEN THE PEOPLE OF THIS COUNTRY DISCOVER THAT IWAKURA AND SATSUMA MURDERED EMPEROR KOMEI AND FORMED THEIR NEW GOVERNMENT UPON THIS VILE CRIME, THEY WILL QUESTION THE LEGITIMACY OF THE PRESENT MIKADO AND COURT, WOULDN'T YOU AGREE?! AND I'D IMAGINE QUITE A FEW DOMAIN LORDS WILL ABANDON YOUR NEW GOVERNMENT AS WELL. ARE YOU PREPARED TO LOSE PUBLIC SUPPORT BEFORE YOU EVEN START?!

HUH...

LADY CHIKAKO...!!

...!

THIS GAMBLE COULD STILL FALL APART.

IF SAIGO DEMANDS PROOF THAT THESE LETTERS WERE HANDWRITTEN BY EMPEROR KOMEI, WHAT WILL WE DO?! HOW DO WE RESPOND IF HE ACCUSES THEM OF BEING FORGERIES?!

AFTER ALL, WE DON'T HAVE TIME TO TRAVEL ALL THE WAY TO KYOTO IN ORDER TO FIND VERIFIED SAMPLES OF THE LATE MIKADO'S HANDWRITING...!

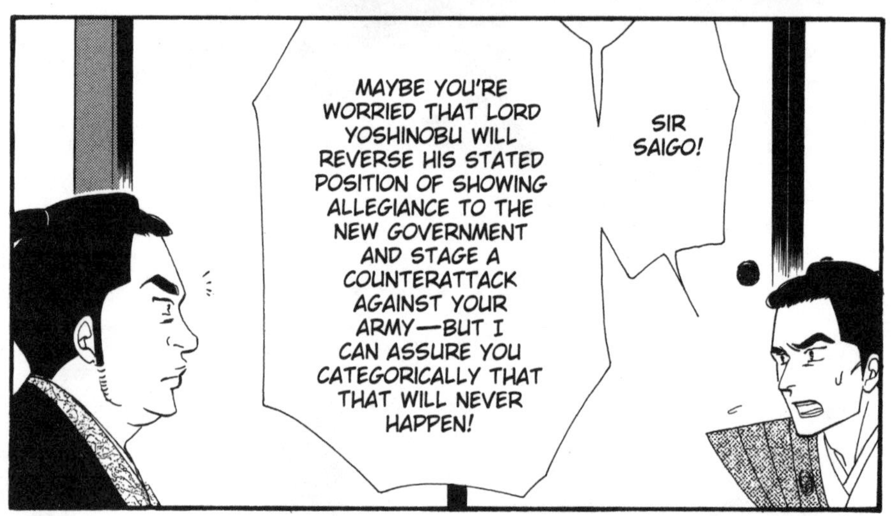

LORD YOSHINOBU IS NOT THE POWER-MAD MONSTER YOU SEEM TO THINK HE IS!

ALL HE CARES ABOUT IS LOOKING GOOD—CUTTING A GOOD FIGURE TO THOSE AROUND HIM. NOW THAT THE NEW GOVERNMENT'S ARMY HAS RAISED THE IMPERIAL BATTLE FLAGS, THE LAST THING LORD YOSHINOBU WILL DO IS ATTACK IT—BECAUSE BEING SEEN TO BE A TRAITOR WOULD MAKE HIM LOOK REALLY, REALLY BAD!

I'VE MET DIRECTLY WITH LORD YOSHINOBU SEVERAL TIMES, AND I PROMISE YOU THAT'S THE TRUTH! SO PLEASE, JUST DON'T TURN THE CITY OF EDO INTO A BATTLEFIELD! THE TOKUGAWA HAVE SURRENDERED! SO PLEASE...!

SIR KATSU. PLEASE.

NOW I REMEMBER CORRECTLY. THE 14TH TOKUGAWA SHOGUN, LORD IEMOCHI...
...WAS A MAN, WASN'T HE?
HUH...?

AFTER ALL, IF THIS PERSONAGE IN FRONT OF ME IS THE SHOGUN'S CONSORT, SHE IS IN FACT AN IMPERIAL PRINCESS, NOT A PRINCE.

SO IT FOLLOWS THAT THE 14TH TOKUGAWA SHOGUN, LORD IEMOCHI, WAS A MAN. IT WOULD NOT MAKE SENSE OTHERWISE, WOULD IT?

COME TO THINK OF IT, THE NAMES OF ALL THE TOKUGAWA SHOGUN RECORDED IN DOCUMENTS OVER THE PAST TWO CENTURIES HAVE BEEN MALE NAMES.

WHICH PROBABLY MEANS THAT IN FACT, ALL OF THOSE SHOGUN WERE ACTUALLY MEN.

IF WE THINK OF IT LIKE THAT, THE HISTORY OF THE TOKUGAWA REIGN IS NOT SHAMEFUL AFTER ALL. SO THEN, THERE IS NO NEED TO KILL LORD YOSHINOBU...

SIR KATSU.
I SHALL AGREE TO YOUR REQUESTS, FOR THE MOST PART. FIRSTLY, LORD YOSHINOBU SHALL BE PLACED IN THE CUSTODY OF MITO, THE DOMAIN OF HIS BIRTH.
SECONDLY, WITH REGARD TO ARMAMENTS AND WARSHIPS, WE SHALL RETURN A SUITABLE QUANTITY TO THE TOKUGAWA FAMILY AFTER REQUISITIONING THEM. AND AS FOR EDO CASTLE, WE ASK THAT IT BE SURRENDERED TO US AFTER ALL THE RETAINERS LIVING THEREIN HAVE VACATED THE PREMISES. DO YOU ACCEDE TO THESE CONDITIONS?

OF COURSE WE DO!
THANK YOU, SIR SAIGO. I APPRECIATE IT!
AND, SIR TANEATSU.
NOW THAT IT HAS BEEN ESTABLISHED THAT ALL THE TOKUGAWA SHOGUN WERE MALE, YOU ARE NO LONGER SIR TENSHO-IN.
I REQUEST THAT, AFTER THE HANDOVER OF EDO CASTLE, YOU RETURN TO SATSUMA AS A SON OF THE SHIMAZU FAMILY.
SAIGO!
SO ARE WE TO UNDERSTAND THAT YOU HAVE CHANGED YOUR MIND ABOUT YOUR PLAN TO ATTACK EDO TOMORROW?
THAT IS CORRECT.

HMPH!

I DON'T CARE HOW INCONVENIENT IT MIGHT BE FOR THE NEW GOVERNMENT THAT WOMEN HAVE BEEN SHOGUN IN THE PAST.

THE CITY OF EDO PROSPERED FOR 200 YEARS UNDER THE STEWARDSHIP OF FEMALE SHOGUN, AND THROUGH THE HARD WORK OF THE WOMEN WHO LIVED HERE. THEY'RE THE ONES WHO BUILT THIS CITY AND MADE IT WHAT IT IS, SEE?

EDO...

YOU AND YOUR MEN CAN DISTORT THE TRUTH ALL YOU WANT. WRITE THE TOKUGAWA WOMEN WHO MADE THIS HISTORY OUT OF YOUR CHRONICLES IF YOU SO DESIRE, IN EXCHANGE FOR THIS—DON'T TOUCH THE CITY OF EDO. NOT ONE SCRATCH!

WHO WOULD HAVE THOUGHT ...

WHO WOULD EVER HAVE THOUGHT IT?

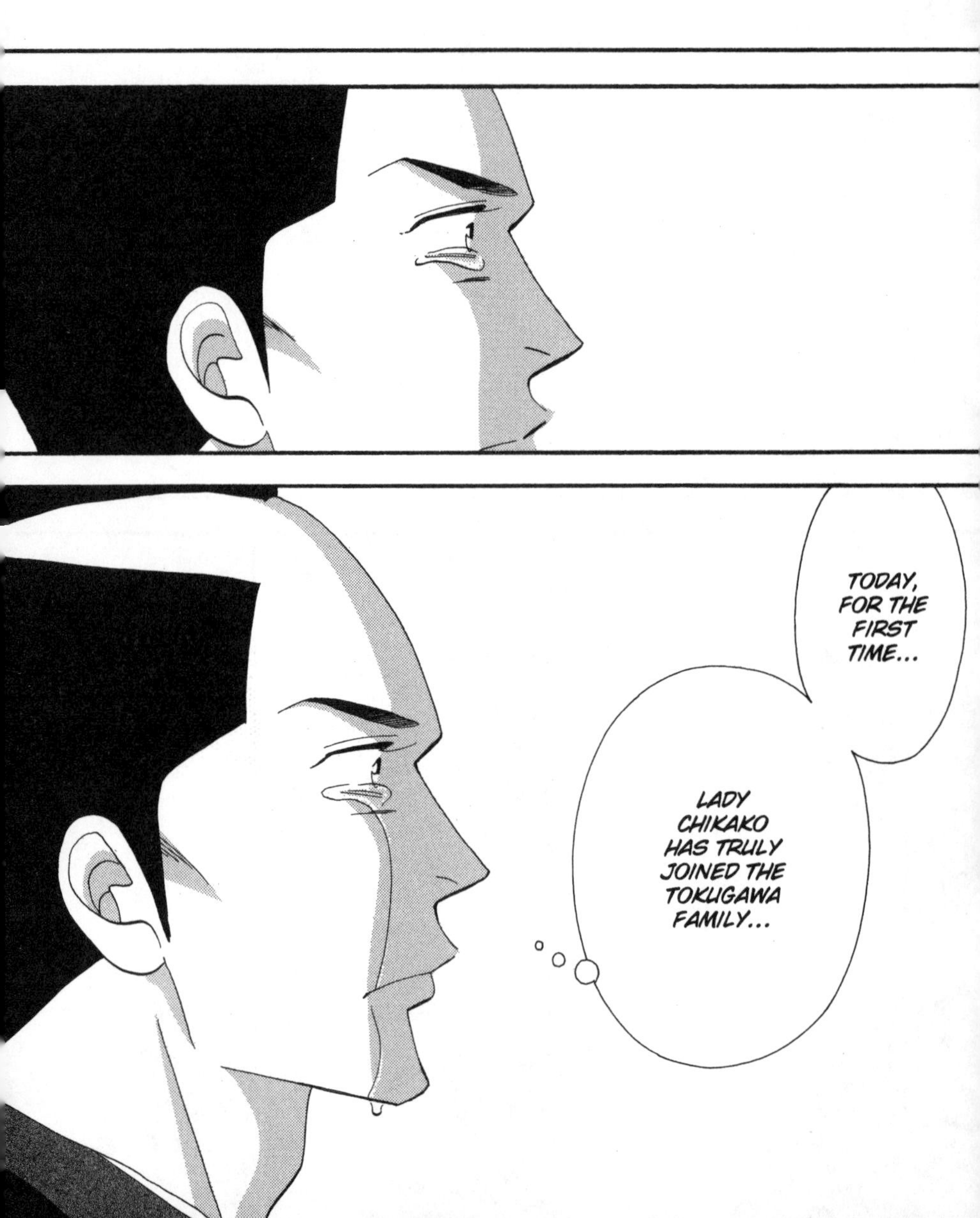

And so it was that the new government's military invasion of Edo was averted, and the bloodless surrender of Edo Castle negotiated.
CERTAINLY.
I GIVE YOU MY WORD.

Ōoku

THE INNER CHAMBERS

Ōoku

THE INNER CHAMBERS

HA! HA! HA! HA! HA!

I ADMIT, I WAS COMPLETELY DUMBFOUNDED FOR ONCE! AND WHO COULD BLAME ME, WHEN A WOMAN I'D NEVER SEEN BEFORE IN MY LIFE JUMPED OUT AND SHOUTED, "KATSU! WHY DON'T YOU SAY SOMETHING?!"

MY WORD... HOW COULD I HAVE KNOWN THAT WOMAN WAS PRINCE KAZU?! I WAS FLABBERGASTED! ABSOLUTELY THUNDERSTRUCK!

BUT TO BE UTTERLY SERIOUS... YOU WERE WITHOUT A DOUBT THE ONE MOST RESPONSIBLE FOR THE FAVORABLE OUTCOME OF THESE NEGOTIATIONS WITH SAIGO, YOUR HIGHNESS.
IF I HAD GONE TO THE PARLEY ALONE, I WOULD NEVER HAVE SUCCEEDED IN PERSUADING HIM TO CONCEDE SO MUCH. IT'S QUITE INCREDIBLE THAT A MAN SO OBDURATE AGREED TO MAKE PEACE ON TERMS SO ADVANTAGEOUS TO THE TOKUGAWA. WHAT A BRAVE, COURAGEOUS PERSON YOU ARE!

KATSU.
WHAT ABOUT THE SURRENDER OF THIS CASTLE? HAS A DATE AND TIME BEEN SET FOR THAT?
YES, SIR. THE DATE HAS BEEN SET FOR THE 11TH DAY OF THE FOURTH MONTH.

PRECEDING THAT, PRINCESS KAZU SHALL VACATE THE PREMISES ON THE NINTH OF THE MONTH, AND SIR TENSHO-IN ON THE TENTH.

SIR TENSHO-IN SHALL MOVE FIRST INTO THE EDO MANSION OF THE SATSUMA DOMAIN, AND FROM THERE RETURN TO SATSUMA AS SIR SHIMAZU TANEATSU. AND YOUR HIGHNESS SHALL STAY AT THE EDO MANSION OF THE TAYASU BRANCH OF THE TOKUGAWA FAMILY FOR THE TIME BEING.

I SAY, THOUGH...

SIR TENSHO-IN, AND SIR TAKIYAMA ALSO... HOW ON EARTH DID YOU MANAGE TO KEEP THE INNER CHAMBERS RUNNING SMOOTHLY WHILE KEEPING THIS TERRIBLE SECRET?!

NOW DO YOU UNDERSTAND, KATSU?! IT WAS VERY DIFFICULT... TRULY, VERY DIFFICULT!

WHAT IS THE MATTER WITH THIS FELLOW, SIR TENSHO-IN?! HE IS AWFULLY FAMILIAR, ISN'T HE?!

YES, MY LADY. THAT IS SIMPLY HIS NATURE, AND OUR LATE LORD IEMOCHI TRUSTED HIM SO MUCH PRECISELY BECAUSE OF HIS CANDOR AND FORTHRIGHTNESS.

HA HA HA! SINCE WE'RE ON THE SUBJECT OF MY IMPUDENCE... LET ME ASK YOU ANOTHER FAVOR!

SIR TENSHO-IN!

SIR TENSHO-IN.
ALTHOUGH WE WERE ABLE TO AVERT AN ASSAULT ON EDO CASTLE BY THE NEW GOVERNMENT'S FORCES, THERE REMAIN MORE THAN A FEW TOKUGAWA RETAINERS WHO ARE STILL ADVOCATING THAT WE GO TO WAR.
I WOULD LIKE TO REQUEST THAT YOU SEND OUT A NOTICE TO ALL TOKUGAWA RETAINERS TO REFRAIN FROM ANY FURTHER ACTS OF FUTILE RESISTANCE AGAINST THE NEW GOVERNMENT, SIR TENSHO-IN!
NOW THAT EDO CASTLE IS WITHOUT A LORD, YOU ARE THE ONLY ONE WHO CAN ACT ON THE SHOGUN'S BEHALF!

Tensho-in issued an unprecedented notice from the Inner Chambers, addressed to all of the Tokugawa retainers.

THIS IS A PERSONAL MESSAGE FROM SIR TENSHO-IN TO ALL OF YOU!

ALTHOUGH THE NEW GOVERNMENT'S ARMY HAS CALLED OFF ITS ATTACK ON EDO CASTLE, WE MUST ENSURE THAT THIS TRUCE IS NOT JEOPARDIZED. FOR THIS REASON, IT IS SIR TENSHO-IN'S HEARTFELT DESIRE THAT ALL OF YOU REMAIN CALM AND COOLHEADED, AND WELCOME THE NEW GOVERNMENT'S ARMY INTO EDO WITH COMPOSURE!

Even so, the wider civil war that Katsu had feared was not averted. It continued in the provinces north of Edo and moved northwards from there all the way up to the Ezo lands of the far north, giving rise to large numbers of dead and wounded.
However, the virtually bloodless handover of the giant metropolis of Edo was a major factor in the rapid transition Japan was able to make from war and upheaval to a new era of modernization.

And, in the short time left until the surrender of Edo Castle, Katsu Kaishu and Tensho-in acted as the Tokugawa shogunate's de facto senior councillor and shogun, respectively.
ALL OF YOU.
AS YOU KNOW, WE WILL BE HANDING EDO CASTLE OVER TO THE NEW GOVERNMENT'S ARMY. NOW THE DATE FOR IT HAS BEEN SET, ON THE 11TH DAY OF THE FOURTH MONTH.
IN THE THREE WEEKS OR SO REMAINING, YOU SHALL GATHER ALL OF YOUR PERSONAL POSSESSIONS AND DEPART THIS CASTLE BY THE TENTH AT THE LATEST.

ALL OF YOU HAVE SERVED THE TOKUGAWA WELL AND FOR A LONG TIME. FOR THIS I THANK YOU MOST SINCERELY, WITH ALL MY HEART.
INDEED, THIS IS THE REASON I HAD ALL OF YOU GATHER HERE TODAY—FROM THE HOUSEBOYS AND OTHERS DEEMED NOT WORTHY OF THE SHOGUN'S SIGHT TO THE MOST HIGH-RANKING OF YOU REMAINING IN THE INNER CHAMBERS. I WANTED TO EXPRESS MY GRATITUDE TO EACH AND EVERY ONE OF YOU IN PERSON.

THANK YOU FOR YOUR SERVICE.

YOU DID WELL, ALL OF YOU!

ALL OF YOU!

THANKS TO THE THOUGHTFUL GENEROSITY OF SIR TENSHO-IN, WE SHALL BE HOLDING THE INNER CHAMBERS' FINAL BLOSSOM VIEWING PARTY ON THE THIRD DAY OF THE FOURTH MONTH.

DUE TO THE IMMINENT PROSPECT OF A MILITARY ATTACK UPON EDO, WE WERE UNABLE TO HOLD SUCH A PARTY DURING THE CHERRY-BLOSSOM SEASON THIS YEAR, BUT FORTUNATELY THE WISTERIA AND AZALEA WILL BE ENTERING THEIR MOMENT OF GREATEST GLORY VERY SOON.

THIS MAY NOT HAVE BEEN POSSIBLE IN OUR HEYDAY, BUT THE DRASTIC REDUCTION IN OUR NUMBERS OVER THE PAST YEAR MEANS THERE ARE JUST 100 OF US LEFT.

ON THAT DAY ALONE, ALL FORMALITIES SHALL BE DROPPED. EVERYONE HERE, REGARDLESS OF RANK, IS INVITED TO TAKE PART IN THE PARTY, FROM HOUSEBOYS AND SENTRIES ON UP.

IT IS SIR TENSHO-IN'S WISH THAT YOU DEPART THE INNER CHAMBERS WITH THE BEAUTIFUL SCENERY OF THE GARDEN OF FUKIAGE IN YOUR MEMORIES. LET THAT BE HIS FINAL GIFT TO YOU ALL.

FISH, EGGS, VEGETABLES, AND SAKE...

SIR TAKIYAMA HAS SAID WE MAY ASSEMBLE THE VERY BEST OF THE BEST FOR THIS FINAL FEAST!

WELL, IF THE INGREDIENTS ARE THE FINEST, WE'VE GOT TO BE THEIR MATCH IN OUR PREPARATION OF THEM. LET'S SHOW THEM WHAT WE'VE GOT!

YES, SIR!!

AFTER ALL, THIS IS THE FIRST AND LAST TIME WE'LL GET TO EAT THE VERY SAME FOOD WE PREPARE FOR SIR TENSHO-IN! YOU KNOW I'M GOING TO TAKE SPECIAL CARE IN MAKING IT!

WHO WOULD'VE THOUGHT THAT DAY WOULD EVER COME?! WE'RE GONNA OUTDO YAOZEN WITH THIS MEAL—IT MIGHT BE THE BEST RESTAURANT IN TOWN, BUT WE'RE THE BEST KITCHEN!

HA HA HA HA HA HA

SIR IKEYA. THESE DAMASK MATS FOR THE FLOWER VIEWING PARTY ARE A BIT FRAYED AT THE EDGES...

HM. THIS IS A SPECIAL PARTY... LET'S MEND ALL THE MATS AND REEMBROIDER THE HOLLYHOCK CREST ON THEM WITH GOLD THREAD.

YES, SIR! WHEN THOSE SATSUMA SOLDIERS ENTER EDO CASTLE, WE'LL SHOW THEM HOW BEAUTIFUL THE TOKUGAWA CREST IS!

THEY'LL PROBABLY BURN THEM ALL RIGHT AWAY, BUT STILL...

IF THERE WERE AN ARBOR HERE, THEN EVEN IF THE DAY OF THE PARTY WERE BRIGHT AND SUNNY, LADY SEIKAN-IN COULD SIT OUTDOORS AND ENJOY THE VIEW IN THE SHADE...
SHALL WE BUILD ONE THEN, SIR KUROKI?!

WHAT?! YOU COULD DO THAT?!
SURE, SIR! THERE ARE A COUPLE OF OTHER HOUSEBOYS BESIDES MYSELF WHO CAN DO CARPENTRY. WE HAVE TWO DAYS, WHICH OUGHT TO BE ENOUGH TIME FOR IT.

WELL THEN, PLEASE DO IT!

VERY WELL, SIR TAKIYAMA. THAT'S 200 OF OUR FINEST SOFT CONFECTIONS AND 500 DRY CONFECTIONS TO BE DELIVERED ON THE MORNING OF THE THIRD.
YES, THAT'S RIGHT.

...

WE HAVE ENJOYED YOUR SWEETS FOR MANY YEARS, SAGAMI-YA.
I VERY MUCH LOOK FORWARD TO SEEING YOUR *WISTERIA* AND *AZALEA* AGAIN—NOT ONLY DELECTABLE IN THE MOUTH, BUT SO BEAUTIFUL TO THE EYE AS WELL.

AS FOR PAYMENT, YOU SHALL BE REIMBURSED IN FULL NOT ONLY FOR THESE SWEETS, BUT FOR EVERYTHING PUT ON THIS ACCOUNT SINCE THE START OF THE YEAR. STOP BY THE ACCOUNTING OFFICE IN THE GREAT CHAMBER ON YOUR WAY OUT ON THE THIRD, AND—
NO, SIR. WE DO NOT REQUIRE PAYMENT.

!

WE AT SAGAMI-YA HAVE PROVIDED THE CASTLE HERE IN CHIYODA WITH SWEETS FOR 150 YEARS, SINCE THE REIGN OF THE EIGHTH TOKUGAWA SHOGUN, LORD YOSHIMUNE.

WHEN I THINK OF THE MANY LONG YEARS OF YOUR KIND PATRONAGE, I COULD NOT POSSIBLY RECEIVE PAYMENT ON THE VERY LAST DAY I DELIVER OUR CONFECTIONS HERE. PLEASE, SIR, I BEG YOU TO ACCEPT THEM AS A TOKEN OF OUR IMMENSE GRATITUDE.

...

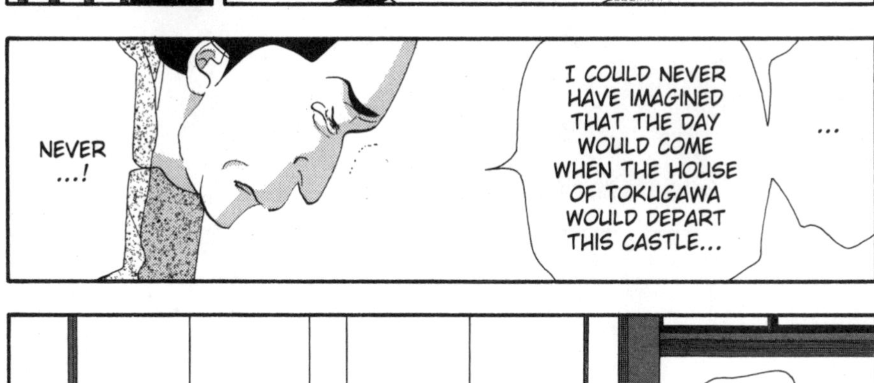

SAGAMI-YA IS BY NO MEANS ALONE IN THOSE SENTIMENTS, SIR. I HAVE HEARD OTHER MERCHANTS WHO PROVISION THE CASTLE SAY MUCH THE SAME.
THEY REFUSE PAYMENT EVEN THOUGH THINGS MUST BE VERY UNCERTAIN FOR THEM AT THIS TIME, WITH THE NEW GOVERNMENT IN TOWN...

WHEN ALL IS SAID AND DONE, NATIVE SONS OF EDO ARE QUITE FOND OF THE TOKUGAWA.
BUT MERCHANTS ARE A PLUCKY LOT. ONCE THE NEW GOVERNMENT IS SETTLED IN, I'M SURE THEY WILL TRADE WITH THEM AS THEY DID WITH US.

THOUGH ACTUALLY, WE HERE IN THE INNER CHAMBERS ARE THE SAME.
ALL OF US MUST MAKE OUR WAY IN THIS NEW AGE THAT HAS DAWNED, MERCHANTS OR NOT. AND SO WE SHALL.
YOU, TOO...

BUT FIRST, THERE IS THE BLOSSOM VIEWING PARTY!
I'M SO LOOKING FORWARD TO IT. I'LL BE MAKING LOTS OF TERU TERU BOZU TO MAKE SURE WE HAVE GOOD WEATHER THAT DAY!

SWIP

OH MY!
SIR TAKIYAMA! YOU HAVE TAKEN THE TROUBLE TO COME HERE?!
I'M SORRY TO BOTHER YOU WHEN YOU'RE BUSY CLEARING THINGS AWAY, FUKAKUSA.
I'VE COME BECAUSE I WANTED TO READ *CHRONICLE OF A DYING DAY* AGAIN, FROM START TO FINISH.

HERE IT IS, SIR. I DON'T EXPECT YOU SHALL FINISH READING IT ALL IN ONE DAY, SO I SHALL BRING THE VOLUMES THAT REMAIN TO YOUR CHAMBERS THIS EVENING.
FUKA-KUSA.
YOU ARE THE ONLY SCRIBE LEFT HERE IN THE INNER CHAMBERS, CORRECT? SO IT FALLS UPON YOU TO RECORD ALL THE EVENTS TAKING PLACE HEREIN, IN THE FINAL VOLUME OF THIS CHRONICLE.

YES, SIR. IT IS AS YOU SAY.

AND YET, FOR ALL YOUR EFFORTS, THE NEW GOVERNMENT'S ARMY WILL PROBABLY BURN IT ALL, DOWN TO THE LAST PAGE, AFTER WE HAND OVER THE CASTLE...

THAT DOES NOT MATTER TO ME.
I SHALL CONTINUE WITH MY DUTIES AS SCRIBE OF THE INNER CHAMBERS UNTIL MY FINAL HOUR HERE, SIR.

*CHRONICLE OF A DYING DAY

CHIRP
CHIRP

CHIRP
CHIRP
CHIRP

MY, LADY NOTO. LOOK AT WHAT A BEAUTIFUL DAY IT IS! AND THE WISTERIA ARE IN FULL BLOOM, TOO!
YES. THANK GOODNESS THE SUN HAS COME OUT FOR THIS FESTIVE OCCASION.

CHIRP
CHIRP

AND THAT'S THE LAST ONE—110 LUNCHEON BOXES FOR THE PARTY, READY!
GOOD WORK, EVERYONE! THEY'VE TURNED OUT WELL!

SIR TAKIYAMA.

ALL THE PREPARATIONS FOR THE FLOWER VIEWING PARTY HAVE BEEN COMPLETED.

I THANK YOU ALL FOR THE TIRELESS EFFORTS YOU HAVE MADE IN PREPARING FOR TODAY'S PARTY!
IT IS A BEAUTIFUL DAY—LET EACH OF YOU FORGET ABOUT YOUR WORRIES AND YOUR WOES TODAY, AND ENJOY YOURSELVES!

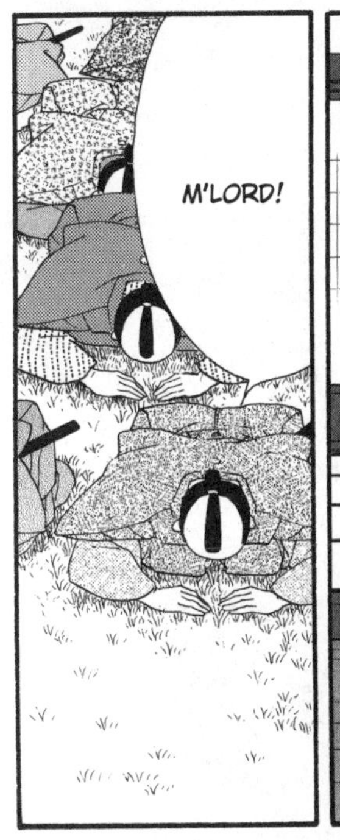
M'LORD!

I'M SORRY, TAKIYAMA. TO THINK YOU NEVER WORE THIS KAMISHIMO UNTIL TODAY, OUT OF CONSIDERATION FOR ME...

OF COURSE I WAS UTTERLY IGNORANT OF THE FACT THAT YOU HAD A KAMISHIMO WITH THIS EXACT SAME FLOWING-WATER PATTERN WHEN I ORDERED ONE FOR MYSELF.

HA HA...

IF I MAY CONFESS, THIS ONE WAS MY VERY FAVORITE. NOW THAT THE CASTLE IS NO LONGER PRESIDED OVER BY A LORD WHO FROWNS UPON LONG HAKAMA, I THOUGHT THIS MIGHT BE MY FINAL CHANCE TO WEAR IT. I BEG YOUR FORGIVENESS FOR BEING SO BOLD.

LADY CHIKAKO!

ATTENTION, ALL!

PAUSE YOUR EATING AND DRINKING, AND LOWER YOUR HEADS FOR THE ENTRANCE OF THE LATE LORD IEMOCHI'S CONSORT!
NO NEED FOR THAT, KUROKI.

RAISE YOUR HEADS, AND CONTINUE ENJOYING YOUR MEAL.

...
THIS...

THIS IS WHO YOU TRULY ARE.
WHAT ARE YOU TALKING ABOUT? I HAVE NEVER BEEN ANYTHING OTHER THAN MYSELF.

MY LADY.

I REALIZE THIS IS EXTREMELY FORWARD OF ME TO SAY, AND I HOPE YOU WILL FORGIVE ME...
BUT YOU ARE...
...SO DAZZLING IN YOUR BEAUTY TODAY THAT IT FEELS AS THOUGH ONCE AGAIN WE HAVE A LORD—THAT IS TO SAY, LADY—REIGNING OVER THESE INNER CHAMBERS.

THANK YOU.

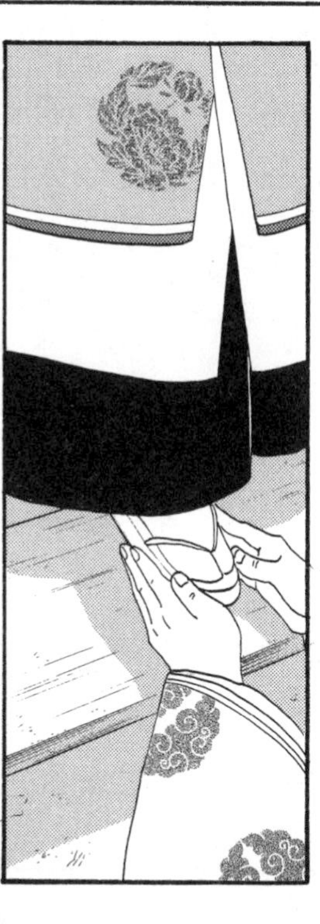

ALL OF YOU.

THANK YOU FOR TAKING SUCH GOOD CARE OF ME DURING MY TIME HERE.

MY LORD IEMOCHI APPRECIATED YOUR SERVICE GREATLY, AND I'M CERTAIN SHE'S FEELING THE SAME WAY RIGHT NOW, UP IN THE HEAVENS.

OHH...
SO THAT'S WHY...ALL THE ROBES WE SEWED FOR OUR LORD'S CONSORT WERE ALWAYS SO NARROW IN BREADTH.
THE PRINCE WAS ACTUALLY A LADY...!

All of the men were remembering the oath they had sealed with blood upon entering into service in the Inner Chambers.

"Never shall I speak of things I have seen or heard inside the Ōoku, nor of anything else that doth take place therein, to my parents, or to my brothers or sisters, or to any other person beyond its walls."

DASH DASH

The next day saw the start of a thorough cleaning of the castle.

NAKAZAWA. TAKE THE BEST INCENSE I HAVE—ALL OF IT—AND PERFUME MY CLOTHES WITH IT, IF YOU WOULD.
ARE YOU PLANNING TO CHANGE INTO OTHER ROBES, SIR?

NO.
BUT ALL THE GARMENTS I HAD MADE FOR ME HERE WILL REMAIN HERE. I WANT THEM TO BE FRAGRANT.

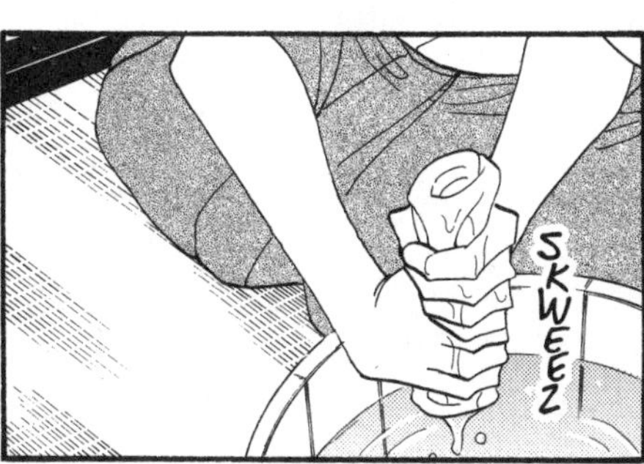
SKWEEZ

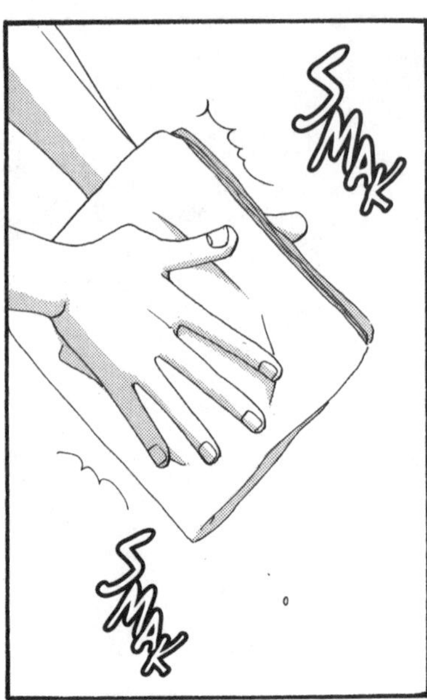
SMAK
SMAK

I'M SORRY, NAKANO. THAT'S WORK THAT OUGHT TO BE DONE BY HOUSEBOYS, NOT A PAGE LIKE YOU.
I DON'T MIND, SIR! EVEN IF THERE WERE A FULL COHORT OF SERVANTS, I WOULDN'T LET ANYONE BUT MYSELF DO THE FINAL CLEANING OF YOUR CHAMBERS.
I AM ALMOST FINISHED, THOUGH, SO IF YOU NEED ANYTHING, I AM AT YOUR SERVICE.

...
WE HAD BEAUTIFUL WEATHER FOR OUR FLOWER VIEWING PARTY, THANKS TO YOUR TERU TERU BOZU. I'M IN YOUR DEBT.

PLEASE, SIR TAKIYAMA! HARDLY! BUT WHAT A SPLENDID PARTY THAT WAS—TRULY GLORIOUS.

SEEING YOU FOR THE FIRST TIME IN THAT GORGEOUS KAMISHIMO WITH THE FLOWING-WATER PATTERN JUST ABOUT MADE ME SWOON. AND THE BEAUTY OF PRINCESS SEIKAN-IN WAS POSITIVELY CELESTIAL...
KNOWING I'LL HAVE THE MEMORY OF THAT DAY IN MY HEART FOR THE REST OF MY LIFE TAKES THE EDGE OFF HAVING TO QUIT THE INNER CHAMBERS... I AM SO BLESSED!

YOU SAID YOU'D GO STAY WITH YOUR UNCLE IN KAWAGUCHI AT FIRST, UPON LEAVING HERE. WILL YOU BE HELPING HIM IN HIS SHOP?
OH...UH, NO! I PLAN TO SEEK A LIVE-IN POST AT SOME OTHER SHOP SOMEWHERE.

THAT MAY BE YOUR PLAN, BUT THE WORLD IS IN TUMULT AT THE MOMENT... IT MAY TAKE SOME TIME BEFORE SOMEONE TAKES YOU IN.
I'LL LAND ON MY FEET, ONE WAY OR ANOTHER. THINGS WILL CALM DOWN SOONER OR LATER.

NAKANO.
YES, SIR?

YOU CAN COME LIVE WITH ME.

BUT...

BUT, SIR...!
WHEN I SAID BEFORE THAT I WISHED TO SERVE AS YOUR PERSONAL ATTENDANT AFTER YOUR DEPARTURE FROM HERE, YOU SAID IT WAS OUT OF THE QUESTION.
SO WHY HAVE YOU CHANGED YOUR MIND...?

AT THAT TIME, I THOUGHT IT WOULD BE BETTER FOR YOU TO LEAVE ME. IT SEEMED A PITY TO LET SOMEONE AS COMPETENT AS YOURSELF END UP AS NOTHING MORE THAN MY VALET.
BUT NOW, EVERYTHING HAS CHANGED...

THE SHOGUNATE THAT I COUNTED UPON TO GIVE YOU A SUCCESSFUL CAREER IS NO MORE.

IF YOUR ONLY OTHER CHOICE IS TO FIND A LIVE-IN POST AT SOME MERCHANT'S SOMEWHERE, THEN IT'S BETTER THAT YOU STAY WITH ME!

SEND YOUR UNCLE A LETTER, QUICKLY. TELL HIM YOU HAVE FOUND A POST AND WILL NOT BE JOINING HIM IN KAWAGUCHI.

WAAAAGH!!

SIR TAKIYAMA... SIR TAKIYAMA...!

S-SIR T-TAKIYAMAAA!

S-S-SIR D-DAGIYABAAA...

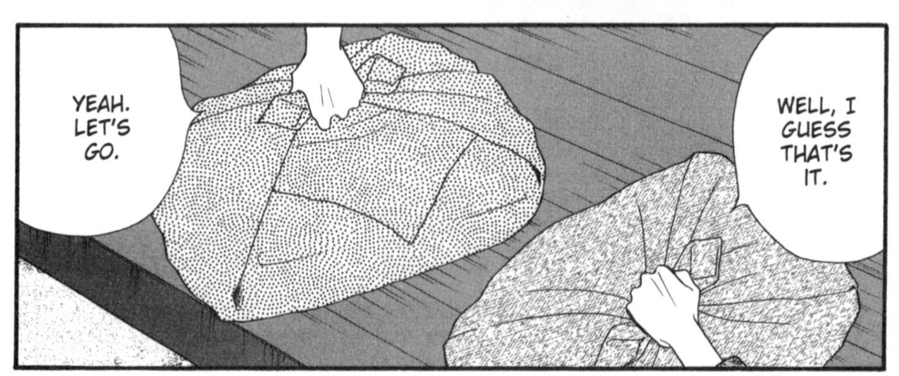

SIR TENSHO-IN.

YOUR PALANQUIN SHALL ARRIVE IN ABOUT AN HOUR. MAY I SUGGEST THAT YOU RETURN TO YOUR CHAMBERS SOON, SIR?
YES, I KNOW I OUGHT TO.

O-MAN'S FAVORITE ...
ALL OF IT... EVERYTHING HERE STARTED WITH SIR O-MAN, DIDN'T IT...?

WASN'T IT LADY KASUGA WHO CREATED THE INNER CHAMBERS?

NO.

NO...

IT WAS HERE IN THE INNER CHAMBERS THAT SIR O-MAN WAS ROBBED OF HIS DREAM OF BECOMING A BUDDHIST PRIEST, AND THEN SUNDERED FROM THE WOMAN HE LOVED, AND UTTERLY DEPRIVED OF ALL HIS PRIDE AS A HUMAN BEING... AND IT WAS THEN, AT THE VERY LIMITS OF HIS SUFFERING, THAT HE BECAME THE FIRST SENIOR CHAMBERLAIN IN CHARGE OF THESE CHAMBERS.

WITHOUT QUESTION, IT WAS SIR MADENOKOJI ARIKOTO WHO WAS THE ORIGIN OF EVERYTHING WE KNOW IN THE INNER CHAMBERS OF EDO CASTLE.

AND SO, IT MAY BE...

IT MAY BE
THAT SIR O-MAN,
MORE THAN
ANYONE ELSE,
WISHED TO SEE
THIS SORROWFUL,
TRAGIC PLACE
CEASE TO EXIST...
AS SOON IT
SHALL.

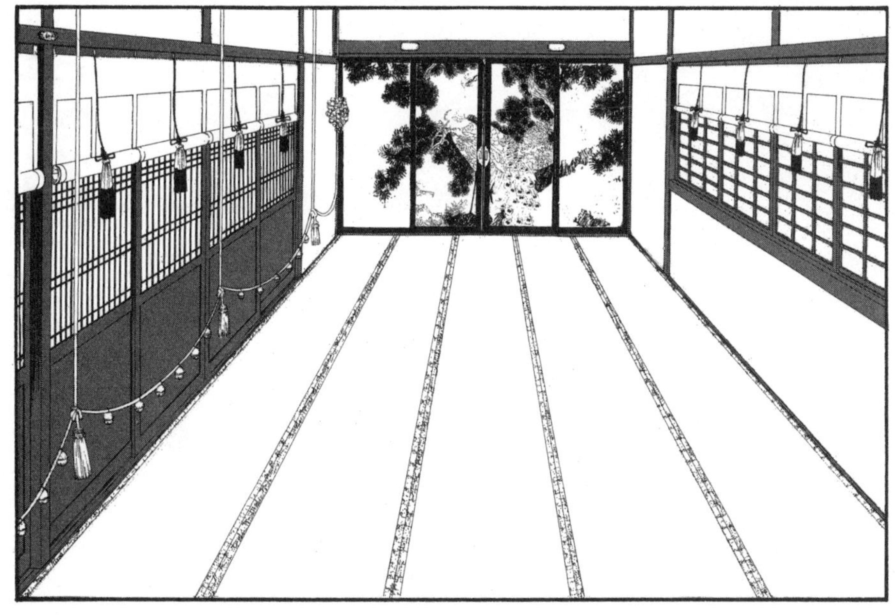

SHRRA
SHRRA
SHRRA
SHRRA
SHRRA

KA-CHAK
BOW YE DOWN ...!!

...FOR THE
ENTRANCE OF
OUR LIEGE!!

NAKANO. I WANT YOU TO ACCOMPANY SIR TENSHO-IN'S PALANQUIN TO THE SATSUMA DOMAIN'S EDO MANSION IN MITA. WAIT FOR ME THERE.

I WILL PAY A COURTESY CALL TO SIR TENSHO-IN SOON, AND THEN YOU WILL ACCOMPANY ME TO MY OWN MANSE IN SHINAGAWA.

VERY WELL, SIR.

And now Tensho-in would be getting into a palanquin for his own departure.

...?!
I DON'T KNOW WHAT YOU'RE TALKING ABOUT!
BUT SIR TAKIYAMA CAME TO SIR TENSHO-IN'S CHAMBERS THE OTHER DAY TO INFORM HIM OF IT, AND LEFT SOME PAPERS WITH HIM AS WELL.

I EXPECT THAT'S WHY HE HAD YOU JOIN OUR PROCESSION TODAY, SO HE COULD INTRODUCE YOU FORMALLY TO SIR TENSHO-IN AS HIS ADOPTED SON AND HEIR?

SIR TAKIYAMA!
I'M SORRY. PLEASE EXCUSE ME!
UH...HEY! WHAT'S THE MATTER?!
SIR TAKIYAMA...!

SIR TAKIYAMA!

SIR TAKIYAMA!

SIR TAKIYAMA!

SHWAP

FORGIVE ME.

I SIMPLY COULD NOT IMAGINE LIVING ANYWHERE IN THIS WORLD, OTHER THAN THIS PLACE...

THESE CEDARWOOD DOORS SHOULD LEAD TO THE INNER CHAMBERS...

HAND ME THE KEY.

SIR!

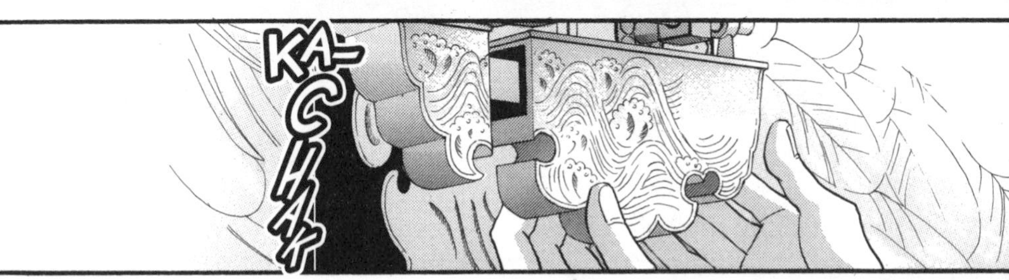

!
WHIFF

EXPENSIVE INCENSE...
I WOULD HAVE EXPECTED A PLACE THAT HOUSED HUNDREDS OF MEN TO BE GRIMIER...MORE OF A MESS...
HUH... SO WE'RE IN THE INNER CHAMBERS ...?

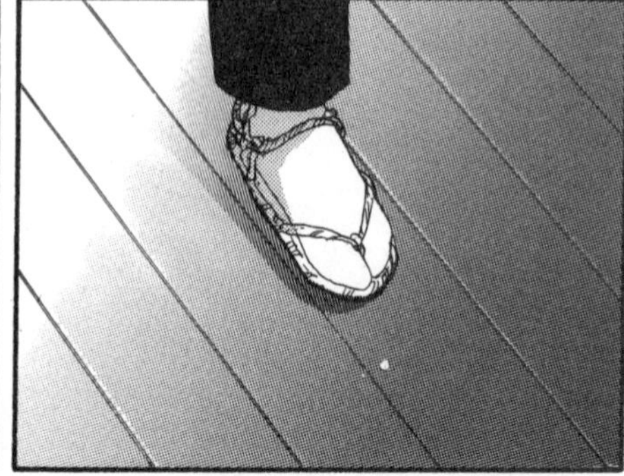

GULP

...
NOT ONE SPECK OF DUST...

WOW... HOW BEAUTIFUL...

BURN THEM.
SIR?!
IT WAS SIR SAIGO'S COMMAND THAT ANYTHING AND EVERYTHING SHOWING THE INNER CHAMBERS TO BE A PLACE THAT HOUSED MEN BE BURNED.

SIR SAIGO WAS ESPECIALLY ADAMANT THAT BOOKS, PAPERS, AND ALL OTHER DOCUMENTS BE DESTROYED, DOWN TO THE LAST PAGE.
MM.
WE NEED TO BURN EVERYTHING IN THIS PLACE BEFORE THE COMMANDER GENERAL, PRINCE ARISUGAWA, FORMALLY TAKES POSSESSION OF THE CASTLE ON BEHALF OF THE GOVERNMENT.

FWOOM

Ōoku
THE INNER CHAMBERS

Ōoku
THE INNER CHAMBERS

Ōoku
THE INNER CHAMBERS

Year 4 of the Meiji era (1871)
ZSSSH

ZSSSH

SIR TANEATSU!

THE WIND IS VERY COLD TODAY. PLEASE RETURN TO YOUR CABIN BEFORE YOU CATCH A CHILL.

MM.

BUT I'M FILLED WITH SUCH HIGH SPIRITS, I CAN'T SIT STILL. I'D LIKE TO STAY OUT ON DECK A LITTLE LONGER.

WHEN I THINK THAT I, WHO UNTIL A FEW SHORT YEARS AGO EXPECTED TO SPEND THE REST OF MY LIFE INSIDE THE INNER CHAMBERS OF EDO CASTLE, AM NOW CROSSING THE SEA TO VISIT A FOREIGN LAND...
NAKAZAWA IS RIGHT, SIR TANEATSU. YOU SHOULD DO AS HE SAYS.

WE STILL HAVE 20-ODD DAYS TO GO BEFORE WE REACH SAN FRANCISCO. IF YOU SHOULD GET ILL NOW, THAT WOULD REALLY MAKE A MESS OF YOUR FIRST VOYAGE OVERSEAS NOW, WOULDN'T IT?

THERE, SIR. YOU HAVE IT ON THE AUTHORITY OF SOMEONE WHO IS CROSSING THE OCEAN FOR THE SIXTH TIME.
I SUPPOSE YOU'RE RIGHT. WE MUST LISTEN TO THE WISDOM OF ONE WHO HAS EXPERIENCE IN THESE MATTERS AND OBEY HIS ADVICE UNTIL OUR RETURN HOME.
EH, TAKIYAMA? I MEAN, SIR TAKIYAMA.

LET ME JUST BE CLEAR, SIRS... MY VOYAGES OVERSEAS WERE MADE FOR THE PURPOSE OF DISCUSSING BUSINESS MATTERS AND WERE NOT SIGHTSEEING PLEASURE TOURS!
YES, OF COURSE! WE KNOW, WE KNOW!

HONESTLY...! I CONFESS I WAS ASTOUNDED WHEN COUNCILLOR SAIGO INFORMED ME THE TWO OF YOU WOULD BE JOINING THIS MISSION AND ASKED ME TO SERVE AS YOUR GUIDE.
I ASSUMED YOU HAD BOTH RETURNED TO SATSUMA—ER, PARDON, IT'S CALLED KAGOSHIMA PREFECTURE NOW—LONG AGO.

BUT WHY DID SAIGO NOT PROVIDE YOU WITH A GUIDE FOR YOUR FIRST OVERSEAS VOYAGE? I WOULD HAVE THOUGHT A MEMBER OF THE SHIMAZU FAMILY WOULD BE TREATED AS A VERY IMPORTANT PERSONAGE BY THE NEW GOVERNMENT.
HE WANTED TO PROVIDE ME WITH AN ESCORT, BUT I REFUSED IT. I STILL CONSIDER MYSELF A MEMBER OF THE TOKUGAWA FAMILY, SO IT DIDN'T SEEM RIGHT.

ACTUALLY, I LEFT THE SHIMAZU FAMILY DIRECTLY AFTER THE NEW GOVERNMENT TOOK POWER, YOU SEE, AND WAS LIVING ON MY SAVINGS. I SPENT MY DAYS LEARNING ENGLISH AT A LANGUAGE ACADEMY, AMONG OTHER THINGS...
YOU KNOW, DOING THIS AND THAT...

MISTER SAIGO MENTIONED THAT YOUR MERCANTILE BUSINESS IS FLOURISHING. HE SAID YOU WERE VERY SUCCESSFUL INDEED.
BUT THEN HOW DID YOU COME UP WITH THE FUNDS FOR THIS VOYAGE?!
I BORROWED THEM! SO, IN ORDER TO PAY THEM BACK, WE NEED TO FIND SOME WAY OF MAKING A LIVING!

...
...
UNTIL...
...HIS SAVINGS WERE ALL GONE...

AND SO WE ARE HOPING YOU MIGHT HIRE US, SIR TAKIYAMA!
...!!

PLEASE, SIR TAKIYAMA!
PLEASE DON'T! HAVING YOU CALL ME "SIR TAKIYAMA" SENDS A NASTY CHILL DOWN MY SPINE FOR SOME REASON!
I'VE BEEN STUDYING ENGLISH WITH AN AMERICAN TEACHER FOR THE PAST THREE YEARS NOW, SO I WON'T HAVE TROUBLE CONVERSING WITH PEOPLE IN THE UNITED STATES. I'M SURE I CAN BE OF SERVICE TO YOU!

I CAN SPEAK ENGLISH MYSELF, YOU KNOW! I HAVE NO NEED FOR AN INTERPRETER!
SIR TAKIYAMA!

REMEMBER YOU OWE SIR TANEATSU A GREAT DEBT!
AND DON'T FOR A MINUTE PRETEND YOU'VE FORGOTTEN ABOUT IT! THINK BACK ON THE EVENTS OF THREE YEARS AGO, AND THEN THINK AGAIN WHETHER GRANTING SIR TANEATSU HIS WISH IS SO GREAT A BURDEN TO YOU!

UH...

S-SIR...
SIR TAKIYAMA! SIR TAKIYAMA!
SIR TAKIYAMAAAAA!
NGH...

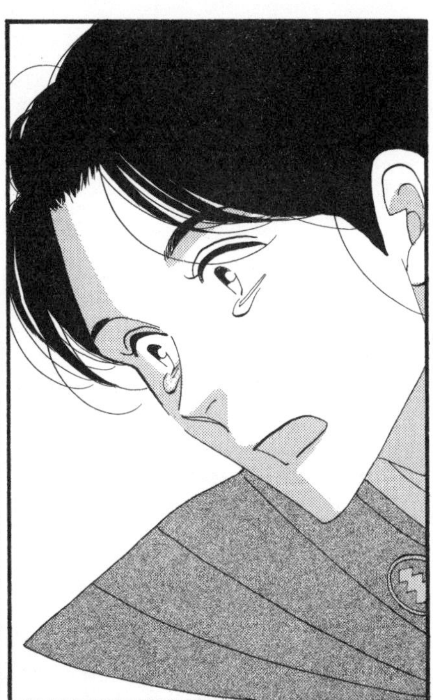

OH! OHHH!!

AHH...!

HE'S ALIVE!!

WHAT THE...?!

OH...! SIR NAKAZAWA!
HE'S...UH, ALIVE!! HE IS STILL WITH US, SIR!
LISTEN WELL, NAKANO!
I'M GOING TO GO NOW TO CALL PEOPLE HERE! WE'RE GOING TO REMOVE A STORM SHUTTER AND PLACE SIR TAKIYAMA ON IT TO CARRY HIM AWAY FROM HERE. UNTIL THEN, I WANT YOU TO PRESS UPON HIS WOUND WITH A CLEAN CLOTH. UNDERSTAND?!

WHAT'S THE MATTER?!

SIR TAKIYAMA. SIR TAKIYAMA... SIR TAKIYAMA ...!
SIR TENSHO-IN!
TAKIYAMA ...!
NAKAZAWA! CARRY HIM STRAIGHT TO MY PALANQUIN!

PLACE TAKIYAMA IN THE PALANQUIN IN MY STEAD, AND BRING HIM TO THE SATSUMA MANSION! I SHALL GO AHEAD TO THE MANSION AND CALL A DOCTOR TO COME THERE. I'LL BE WAITING FOR YOU!

!!

S-SIR TANEATSU?!
WHAAT ?!

KLOP KLOP KLOP KLOP
KLOPKLOP

WHOA, WHOA, WHOA!

SIR TANEATSU !! WHAT ON EARTH ...?!
SAIGO! A WOUNDED MAN WILL BE BROUGHT HERE SHORTLY!

HE IS SOMEONE VERY CLOSE TO ME. I WANT YOU TO SEND FOR A DOCTOR OF WESTERN MEDICINE IMMEDIATELY!
PLEASE! I WANT MORE THAN ANYTHING TO SAVE THIS MAN'S LIFE. I NEED A GOOD DOCTOR— THE BEST YOU CAN FIND!

THE OPERATION WAS A SUCCESS.
BUT THE WOUND WAS NOT MORTAL, ANYWAY. HE OUGHT TO BE UP AND WALKING AROUND IN A FORTNIGHT OR SO.

THIS POCKET WATCH WAS INSIDE THE BOSOM OF HIS KIMONO.

HIS SWORD MUST HAVE HIT THE POCKET WATCH AND BEEN DEFLECTED. WE MIGHT VERY WELL SAY THIS WATCH SAVED HIS LIFE.

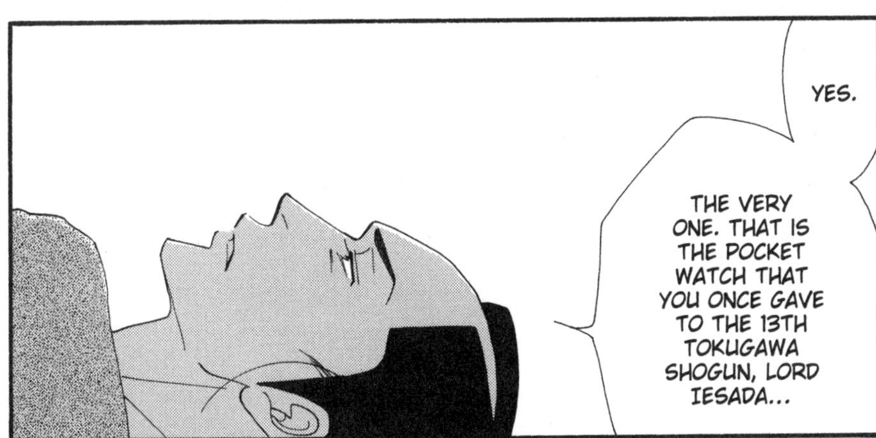

SIR TENSHO-IN. I HOPE YOU WILL FORGIVE ME FOR RETURNING THIS POSSESSION OF YOUR BELOVED LADY TO YOU IN THIS STATE.

EVER SINCE THE DAY YOU FLUNG IT BACK AT ME, I KEPT THIS POCKET WATCH SECRETED INSIDE THE BOSOM OF MY KIMONO, READY TO BE RETURNED TO YOU AT THE FIRST OPPORTUNITY. INSTEAD, IT FOILED ME...

TAKIYAMA.
IF THAT BE SO, WE MAY TAKE IT AS HER WAY OF TELLING YOU IT WAS TOO SOON FOR YOU TO BE JOINING HER THERE...

GO BACK WHERE YOU CAME FROM, YOU FOOL!!

PFF...
HA HA!
I CAN JUST HEAR HER...AND SEE HER, TOO...

...
COME! YOU MAY ENTER NOW. I'M SORRY I KEPT YOU WAITING.

...

...
I HEARD YOUR VOICE.

I HAD INTENDED TO FOLLOW THE PROPER FORMALITIES AND DO IT RIGHT—CLEANSE MYSELF, CHANGE INTO A WHITE KIMONO, ALL OF IT.

BUT YOU UNDERSTOOD WHAT I MEANT TO DO MUCH SOONER THAN I HAD EVER IMAGINED YOU WOULD. I HEARD YOUR VOICE, FAR AWAY, CALLING MY NAME... AND FELT I HAD TO RUSH...

I DIDN'T EVEN HAVE TIME TO SLIP MY ARMS OUT OF MY KIMONO TO EXPOSE MY MIDRIFF. I COMPLETELY FORGOT THAT I HAD THAT POCKET WATCH IN MY BOSOM. I JUST PLUNGED THE SWORD IN AND DID THE BEST I COULD...WHICH IS TO SAY, I BOTCHED IT COMPLETELY.

HONESTLY...

YOU ARE JUST TOO ATTENTIVE...

NAKA-NO.

YOUR HABITUAL THOUGHTFULNESS SAVED YOUR FATHER'S LIFE. TAKIYAMA IS VERY FORTUNATE INDEED TO HAVE A SON LIKE YOU.

TAKIYAMA!

IT WAS THANKS TO NAKANO'S UNSWERVING DEVOTION THAT YOU HAVE BEEN GRANTED A SECOND LEASE ON LIFE. SO DON'T YOU EVEN THINK FOR A MOMENT THAT IT IS SHAMEFUL YOU SURVIVED!

NOT ONLY THAT, WHAT YOU DID WAS A BLOT UPON THE HONOR OF KATSU, WHO STAKED HIS VERY LIFE UPON A BLOODLESS TRANSFER OF EDO CASTLE! I ABSOLUTELY FORBID YOU FROM TRYING AGAIN TO FOLLOW THE TOKUGAWA CLAN INTO OBLIVION!

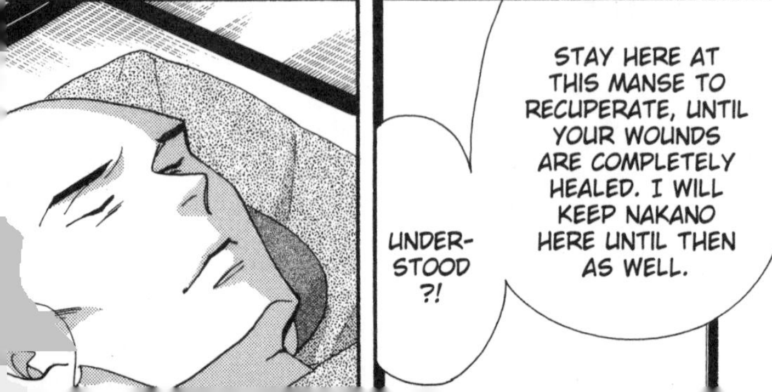

HA HA...!

LADY CHIKAKO! AND KUROKI TOO...!
IT'S BEEN JUST TWO WEEKS, AND YET IT FEELS SO MUCH LONGER. HOW GOOD IT IS TO SEE YOU!

I AM EXCEEDINGLY HONORED AND DELIGHTED TO HAVE THIS PLEASURE, YOUR HIGHNESS.
OH PLEASE, DON'T BOW DOWN TO ME! IT WILL ONLY MAKE YOUR WOUND POP OPEN. I MUST SAY, YOU REALLY ARE A THORN IN MY SIDE TO THE LAST. HERE I'D THOUGHT THAT, ONCE I'D LEFT THE INNER CHAMBERS, I'D NEVER HAVE TO SEE YOU AGAIN!

DON'T FLATTER YOURSELF THAT I'VE COME TO SEE HOW YOU'RE RECOVERING. I HAVE SOMETHING TO TELL YOU, THAT'S ALL.
TAKI-YAMA!
DON'T BE SO SELFISH! I WILL NOT COUNTENANCE THE LIKES OF YOU GETTING TO SEE LORD IEMOCHI AGAIN BEFORE I DO!

I HEARD FROM MY BROTHER THAT YOUR WOUND IS NOT DEEP, SIR TAKIYAMA, AND THAT YOU WILL MAKE A FULL RECOVERY. HOW VERY FORTUNATE, SIR.

MM.
I CONFESS, THOUGH, THAT I WAS ASTONISHED TO DISCOVER THAT THE DOCTOR WHO TREATED TAKIYAMA WAS YOUR ELDER BROTHER, KUROKI. WHAT A SMALL WORLD!
INDEED, SIR.

SIR TENSHO-IN...ER, NO, SIR TANEATSU.

YOU SEE, MY BROTHER WAS PART OF THE TEAM OF WESTERN-MEDICINE PHYSICIANS WHO ATTENDED LORD IESADA WHEN SHE COLLAPSED. HE WAS ALSO PRESENT WHEN SHE DREW HER FINAL BREATH.

THE NEXT TIME MY BROTHER COMES HERE TO EXAMINE SIR TAKIYAMA, WOULD IT BE POSSIBLE FOR YOU AND HIM TO SPEND SOME TIME TOGETHER ALONE?

?

THANK YOU, KUROKI.
PLEASE TELL YOUR BROTHER THAT I WOULD INDEED LIKE VERY MUCH TO HEAR WHAT HE HAS TO TELL ME, THE NEXT TIME HE IS HERE.
VERY WELL, SIR. I WILL DO SO.

AS FOR YOURSELF, KUROKI... YOU INTEND TO STAY IN THE SERVICE OF PRINCESS KAZU, I GATHER.

YES, SIR.
WITH HER PERMISSION, I WILL ATTEND HER HIGHNESS AS A COURTIER THIS TIME, NOT A SAMURAI...
BUT MY WISH IS TO SERVE PRINCESS KAZU TO THE END OF MY DAYS, SIR.

WHAAT?!
I, STAND IN FOR YOU, SIR TENSHO-IN?! FOR YOUR OFFICIAL PHOTOGRAPHIC PORTRAIT?!

OH MY...! THEY SAY THAT WHEN YOUR IMAGE SHOWS UP IN A PHOTOGRAPH, YOUR SOUL LEAVES YOUR BODY AND SLIPS INTO THE IMAGE... WILL YOU BE ALL RIGHT?
THAT IS PURE SUPERSTITION, LADY TSUCHIMIKADO!
BUT I WISH TO BE EXCUSED FOR ANOTHER REASON—THE PRESUMPTION OF IT! HOW DARE I STAND IN FOR SOMEONE OF YOUR STATURE?!
NOTO, ER... SORRY, YOU ARE O-SHIMA AGAIN NOW. PLEASE RECONSIDER!

IT'S SAIGO'S IDEA TO HAVE A PHOTOGRAPH SERVE AS EVIDENCE THAT LORD IESADA'S CONSORT WAS A WOMAN.
THE IDEA IS A GOOD ONE, BUT THEN WE MUST FIND SOMEONE WITH WHOM THE SECRET WOULD BE SAFE, AND MOREOVER, WHO WOULD BE CREDIBLE IN THE PART.

AS I WAS MULLING IT OVER, I REMEMBERED YOU. SHIMA! YOU WOULD BE IDEAL FOR THE TASK!
NO, SIR! HOW COULD YOU SUGGEST SUCH A THING?! I COULD NEVER BE EQUAL TO IT!

I DISAGREE WHOLEHEARTEDLY. YOU SERVED LORD IEMOCHI AT CLOSE QUARTERS FROM CHILDHOOD, AND AGAIN AS AN ADULT. IN THE HISTORY OF THE TOKUGAWA SHOGUNATE, THERE WERE MORE THAN A FEW EXAMPLES OF PRIVY COUNCILLORS RISING TO THE RANK OF SENIOR COUNCILLOR. WHO KNOWS, IN DIFFERENT TIMES YOU MIGHT HAVE DONE SO YOURSELF!
A WOMAN WHO COULD HAVE BECOME A SENIOR COUNCILLOR IS MORE THAN SUITABLE TO STAND IN FOR THE SHOGUN'S CONSORT!

And so it was that a few photographs remain to this day as portraits of Tensho-in, who came to be known as Atsuhime, or Lady Atsu.

PLEASE DO.

I'VE NEVER TOLD KUROKI THIS, BUT THE TRUTH IS THAT I HAVE NEVER BEEN CONVINCED BY THE ACCOUNTS I WAS GIVEN ABOUT MY LORD'S DEMISE.

OH...

...

I SEE.
THAT IS THE SUSPICION YOU HAVE HARBORED FOR ALL THESE YEARS.

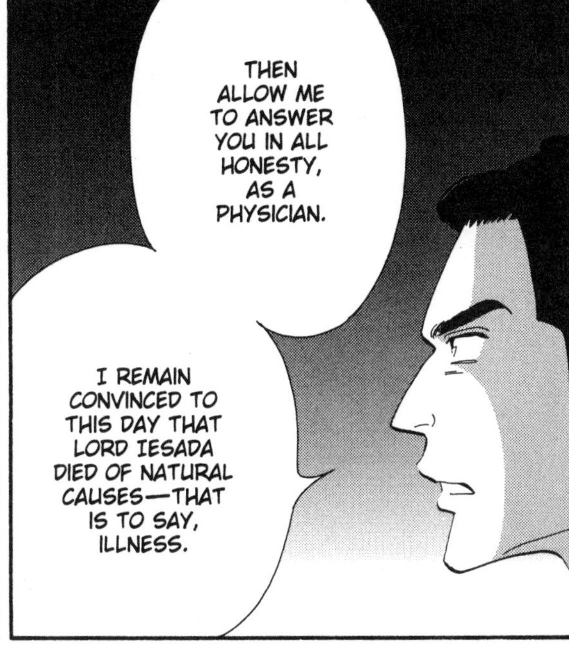
THEN ALLOW ME TO ANSWER YOU IN ALL HONESTY, AS A PHYSICIAN.
I REMAIN CONVINCED TO THIS DAY THAT LORD IESADA DIED OF NATURAL CAUSES—THAT IS TO SAY, ILLNESS.

WHEN HER HIGHNESS SPOKE HER LAST WORDS, HER FACE SHOWED THE SYMPTOMS OF JAUNDICE—THAT IS TO SAY, HER SKIN HAD TURNED A YELLOW COLOR.

THIS IS A TYPICAL SYMPTOM IN PATIENTS WHOSE LIVERS ARE DISEASED...

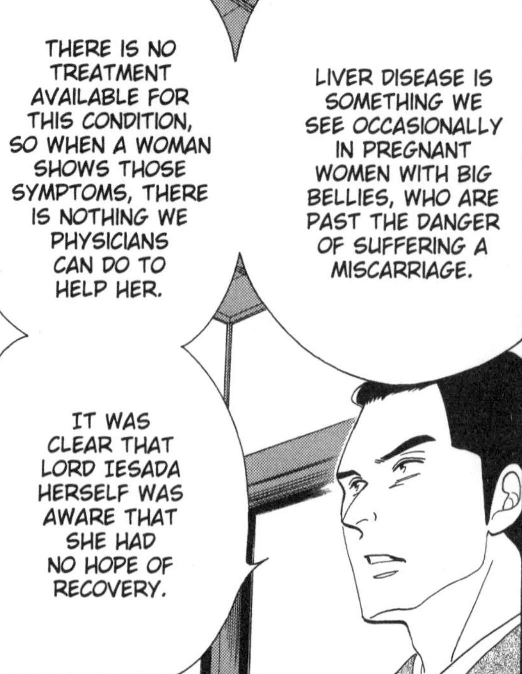

...
I SEE...

TANEATSU...
FORGIVE ME.
I WON'T BE GRANTED ONE LAST SIGHT OF YOU, OR THE CHANCE TO SHOW YOU OUR CHILD...
AND I'M SO SORRY FOR YOU, POOR CHILD IN MY BELLY, THAT I CAN'T GIVE BIRTH TO YOU...
AND YET YOU, WHO ARE CHEATED OF LIFE, ARE WILLING TO ACCOMPANY YOUR MOTHER TO THE OTHER WORLD, WITHOUT A BEGRUDGING WORD...
WHAT A GOOD CHILD YOU ARE...

I SEE.
SO THAT'S HOW IT WAS...

THANK YOU FOR TELLING ME THIS. I'M SO GRATEFUL.

NOW I CAN...

FINALLY, AFTER ALL THIS TIME...

I MEAN, REALLY, SIR TAKIYAMA—THAT WAS AN AWFUL THING TO DO, FIRST ADOPTING ME AS YOUR SON WITHOUT A WORD TO ME, AND THEN TRYING TO KILL YOURSELF WITHOUT A WORD TO ME!

I'VE ALREADY LOST TWO PARENTS AT ONCE IN A FIRE. YOU KNEW THAT, SIR TAKIYAMA, AND YET YOU TRIED TO MAKE ME GO THROUGH THE LOSS OF A PARENT A SECOND TIME!

I LOST MY PARENTS BEFORE I COULD BE A GOOD SON TO THEM.

NOW THAT YOU HAVE GIVEN ME THE HONOR OF BECOMING MY FATHER, PLEASE LET ME TAKE GOOD CARE OF YOU AND BE THE SON I WISH TO BE.

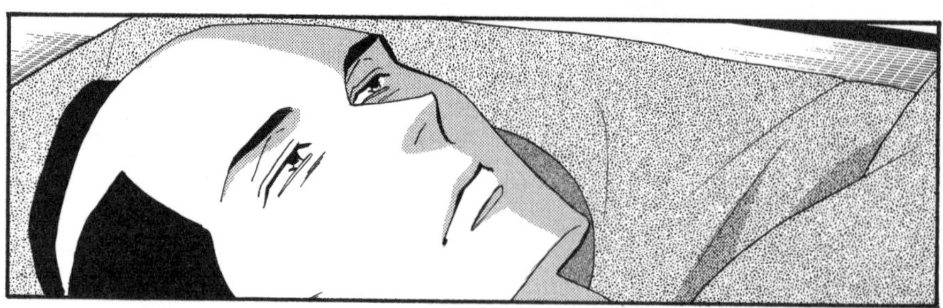

I DON'T KNOW WHAT TO DO WITH MYSELF, NOW THAT I AM NO LONGER IN THE INNER CHAMBERS.

YOU CAN DO ANYTHING! YOU CAN GO FISHING, OR GROW BONSAI, OR ANYTHING YOU LIKE!

...
MAYBE YOU'RE RIGHT. I HAVE RETIRED FROM MY WORK, AND I SHOULD SIMPLY ENJOY MY REMAINING DAYS DOING THINGS THAT GIVE ME PLEASURE.

YES!

HA HA, WHAT A SIMPLE SOLUTION TO MY DILEMMA. HOW SILLY OF ME NOT TO THINK OF IT.
ENJOY MY RETIREMENT, HUH...

OF COURSE ...

THAT'S WHAT YOU SAID WHEN YOU WERE RECUPERATING, FATHER, BUT LOOK AT YOU NOW—YOU'RE A SUCCESSFUL INTERNATIONAL BUSINESSMAN WHO HAS ALREADY CROSSED THE OCEAN SEVERAL TIMES!

NAKANO?!
MY NAME IS TAKIYAMA SINCE MY ADOPTION, BUT PLEASE CALL ME BY MY PERSONAL NAME, WHICH IS KICHIBE.
HE GREW SOME MORE SINCE YOU LAST SAW HIM, THANKS TO WHICH WE CAN DO BUSINESS WITH AMERICANS WITHOUT THEM LOOKING DOWN ON US AS LITTLE PEOPLE.

BUT REALLY, CALLING ME A "SUCCESSFUL INTERNATIONAL BUSINESSMAN" IS OVERDOING IT. MY INTENTION WAS THAT MY FIRST VOYAGE OVERSEAS WOULD BE A SIGHTSEEING TRIP, TAKEN PURELY FOR PLEASURE.
BUT THEN, A TEXTILE WHOLESALER I MET IN YOKOHAMA, WHERE I WAS PLAYING AT BEING AN INTERPRETER JUST TO FILL MY TIME, ASKED ME TO ACCOMPANY HIM TO AMERICA FOR SOME BUSINESS NEGOTIATIONS.

WHILE THERE, I HAPPENED TO VISIT AN AMERICAN AT HIS HOME, AND WHAT SHOULD I SEE PROUDLY DISPLAYED ON THE WALL BUT THE LABEL FROM A BOX OF EXPORTED JAPANESE TEA! IT WAS JUST A CHEAP WOODBLOCK PRINT, WHICH THE MAN HAD CAREFULLY REMOVED AND FRAMED.

I COULDN'T HELP BUT TELL HIM THERE WERE FAR SUPERIOR WOODBLOCK PRINTS IN JAPAN AND THAT I WOULD BRING HIM SOME ON MY NEXT VISIT...

I used to work in the shogun's palace, so I have a good eye for art.

Oh! The shogun?!

Yes, the shogun!

AND THEN, LOOK... SEE THOSE GIRLS OVER THERE?

THEY BELONG TO THE FIRST COHORT OF JAPANESE GIRLS BEING SENT ABROAD FOR THEIR EDUCATION.
MAYBE IT'S SIMPLY A MATTER OF NATIONAL PRIDE, BUT OUR GOVERNMENT IS SENDING THEM TO AMERICA FOR YEARS OF STUDY WITH NOTHING BUT KIMONO TO WEAR. WELL, JAPANESE WOMEN MAY STILL BE WEARING KIMONO NOW...

...BUT I EXPECT THE DAY WILL SOON COME WHEN THEY SWITCH TO WESTERN DRESSES AS WELL.
SO I AM PLANNING TO START IMPORTING LADIES' ACCESSORIES AND ACCOUTREMENTS IN THE NEAR FUTURE, AS THAT IS SURE TO BE A BURGEONING MARKET.

HMMM... HE'S RIGHT. I DON'T KNOW ABOUT SIR TENSHO-IN, BUT NAKAZAWA IS QUICK-WITTED AND CAPABLE. I COULD SEE FINDING A USE FOR HIM...

AH! SO YOU'RE PLANNING TO EXPAND THE SCOPE OF YOUR PRESENT BUSINESS— SO SURELY YOU WILL NEED SOME EXTRA HANDS!
SIR TAKIYAMA! I CAN'T SPEAK ENGLISH THE WAY SIR TANEATSU CAN, BUT I EXPECT YOU WOULD FIND ME THE MORE USEFUL OF THE TWO!

WOOSH

VERY WELL! YOU ARE BOTH HIRED. NAKAZAWA, YOU SHALL BE EMPLOYED AS MY ASSISTANT!
Sir Tensho-in is just extra!
YAAAAY!
Of course!

AGH ...!

FATHER! I'LL GO—
NO NEED, KICHIBE. LET'S SET ONE OF OUR NEW EMPLOYEES TO WORK. TANEATSU!! RETRIEVE MY HAT!
YES, SIR! AT ONCE, SIR TAKIYAMA!

HERE YOU ARE, SIR. I'M GLAD IT DIDN'T FALL INTO THE WATER.
THANK YOU SO MUCH. THAT BELONGS TO MY BOSS.

YOU ARE QUITE A BIT SMALLER THAN THOSE OTHER YOUNG LADIES OVER THERE, AND YET YOU'RE GOING WITH THEM TO STUDY IN AMERICA.
WHAT A TREMEN-DOUSLY BRAVE AND SPLENDID THING THAT IS.

I'M NOT CRYING BECAUSE I MISS MY FAMILY.
ALL THE OTHER MISSES KEEP SAYING, "POOR O-UME, BEING SENT ABROAD AT THE AGE OF SIX... YOUR FATHER MUST BE A CRUEL AND HEARTLESS MAN."

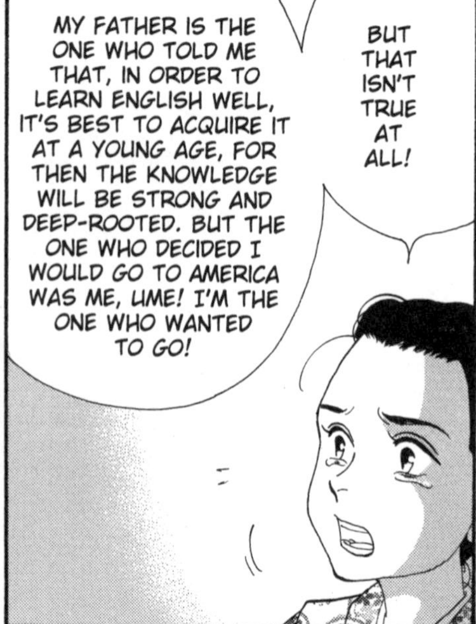
BUT THAT ISN'T TRUE AT ALL!
MY FATHER IS THE ONE WHO TOLD ME THAT, IN ORDER TO LEARN ENGLISH WELL, IT'S BEST TO ACQUIRE IT AT A YOUNG AGE, FOR THEN THE KNOWLEDGE WILL BE STRONG AND DEEP-ROOTED. BUT THE ONE WHO DECIDED I WOULD GO TO AMERICA WAS ME, UME! I'M THE ONE WHO WANTED TO GO!

MY GOOD-NESS ...!
YOU ARE... EXTRAORDINARY. I CAN SCARCELY BELIEVE THOSE WORDS WERE SPOKEN BY A SIX-YEAR-OLD GIRL. I NOW UNDERSTAND VERY WELL WHY YOUR FATHER ALLOWED YOU TO SAIL TO AMERICA FOR YOUR STUDIES!

NO DOUBT YOUR FATHER FELT THAT LETTING YOUR INTELLIGENCE GO UNDEVELOPED WOULD BE A LOSS NOT JUST FOR YOURSELF BUT FOR THE WORLD, FOR SURELY YOU WILL BE SOMEONE GREAT IN THE FUTURE. AND THAT IS WHY HE LET YOU GO TO AMERICA TO STUDY, UME-SAN.

...
BUT I'M A GIRL.
ALL THE OTHER MISSES SAY THAT THE REASON WE ARE GOING TO AMERICA IS TO LEARN ENOUGH TO SUPPORT THE GREAT MEN WHO ARE MOVING OUR COUNTRY FORWARD...AS THEIR WIVES.

NO!
THAT IS NOT TRUE. YOU YOURSELVES WILL BECOME INFLUENTIAL PEOPLE WHO WILL MOVE OUR COUNTRY FORWARD.
YOU WILL! I CAN SEE THAT, PERFECTLY CLEARLY!

IN FACT...

THIS IS A SECRET THAT NOBODY MUST KNOW, BUT I WILL SHARE IT WITH ONLY YOU, UME-SAN.

I AM A MAN, BUT A LONG TIME AGO I WAS THE SHOGUN'S CONSORT.

YOU SEE, IN THE JAPAN OF OLD...
...FOR MANY GENERATIONS, THE SHOGUN WAS A WOMAN...

Ōoku

THE INNER CHAMBERS

The
End

Ōoku: The Inner Chambers

VOLUME 19 · END NOTES

by Akemi Wegmüller

Page 10, panel 3 · Koku

A Japanese unit of dry measurement equivalent to about five bushels.

Page 57, panel 4 · Hyo

A *hyo* is the same as a *tawara*, which is a cylindrical straw sack holding about 60 kilograms of rice.

Page 64, panel 3 · Outside domain

A domain that declared fealty to the shogunate after the Battle of Sekigahara and was therefore never considered a true vassal.

Page 135, panel 2 · Teru teru bozu

Paper dolls made as talismans for bringing good weather. The phrase literally means "sunshine monks."

Page 143, panel 1 · Kamishimo

Kamishimo are formal attire. The word literally means "upper and lower" and is an ensemble that goes over the kimono for formal occasions. The upper section is a sleeveless robe with wide starched shoulders. The lower section is an undivided *hakama*, or skirtlike garment.

Creator Biography

Fumi Yoshinaga

Fumi Yoshinaga is a Tokyo-born manga creator who debuted in 1994 with *Tsuki to Sandaru* (*The Moon and the Sandals*). Yoshinaga has won numerous awards, including the 2009 Osamu Tezuka Cultural Prize for *Ōoku*, the 2002 Kodansha Manga Award for her series *Antique Bakery*, and the 2006 Japan Media Arts Festival Excellence Award for *Ōoku*. She was also nominated for the 2008 Eisner Award for Best Writer/Artist.

Ōoku

THE INNER CHAMBERS

Ōoku: The Inner Chambers
Vol. 19

VIZ Signature Edition

Story and Art by Fumi Yoshinaga

Translation & Adaptation/Akemi Wegmüller
Touch-up Art & Lettering/Monaliza De Asis
Design/Yukiko Whitley
Editor/Pancha Diaz

Printed in Canada

Published by VIZ Media, LLC
P.O. Box 77010
San Francisco, CA 94107

10 9 8 7 6 5 4 3 2 1
First printing, March 2022

PARENTAL ADVISORY
ŌOKU: THE INNER CHAMBERS is rated M for Mature and is recommended for ages 18 and up. Contains violence and attempted suicide.

viz.com

VIZ SIGNATURE

vizsignature.com

THIS IS THE LAST PAGE.

Ōoku: The Inner Chambers has been printed in the original Japanese format in order to preserve the orientation of the original artwork.